PRIMARY MATHEMATICS 4B
TEXTBOOK

SingaporeMath.com Inc

Marshall Cavendish
Education

Marshall Cavendish Education
A member of Times Publishing Limited
Times Centre, 1 New Industrial Road, Singapore 536196
Customer Service Hotline: (65) 6213 9106
E-mail: fps@sg.marshallcavendish.com
Website: www.marshallcavendish.com/education/sg

Distributed by
SingaporeMath.com Inc
404 Beavercreek Road #225
Oregon City, OR 97045
U.S.A.
Website: http://www.singaporemath.com

First published 2003
Reprinted 2003, 2004, 2005 (twice), 2006 (twice)

ISBN 981-01-8507-3
ISBN 978-981-01-8507-7

Printed in Singapore by Times Graphics Pte Ltd

Illustrated by: Paul Yong

ACKNOWLEDGEMENTS

Our special thanks to Richard Askey, Professor of Mathematics (University of Wisconsin, Madison), Yoram Sagher, Professor of Mathematics (University of Illinois, Chicago), and Madge Goldman, President (Gabriella and Paul Rosenbaum Foundation), for their indispensable advice and suggestions in the production of Primary Mathematics (U.S. Edition).

PREFACE

Primary Mathematics (U.S. Edition) comprises textbooks and workbooks. The main feature of this package is the use of the **Concrete ➡ Pictorial ➡ Abstract** approach. The students are provided with the necessary learning experiences beginning with the concrete and pictorial stages, followed by the abstract stage to enable them to learn mathematics meaningfully. This package encourages active thinking processes, communication of mathematical ideas and problem solving.

The textbook comprises 6 units. Each unit is divided into parts: ❶, ❷, . . . Each part starts with a meaningful situation for communication and is followed by specific learning tasks numbered 1, 2, . . . The textbook is accompanied by a workbook. The sign ⌐Workbook Exercise⌐ is used to link the textbook to the workbook exercises.

Practice exercises are designed to provide the students with further practice after they have done the relevant workbook exercises. Review exercises are provided for cumulative reviews of concepts and skills. All the practice exercises and review exercises are optional exercises.

The color patch ■ is used to invite active participation from the students and to facilitate oral discussion. The students are advised not to write on the color patches.

CONTENTS

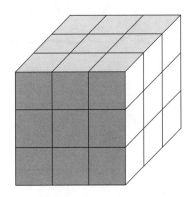

Decimals

1 Tenths

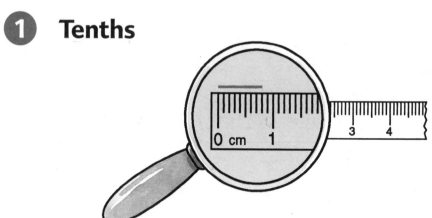

The length of the string is $\frac{8}{10}$ cm or 0.8 cm.

$0.8 = \frac{8}{10}$

We read 0.8 as **zero point eight**.

The weight of the bread is 0.8 kg.

The amount of water is 0.8 ℓ.

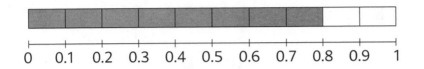

0.8 is 8 tenths.

Numbers like 0.1 and 0.8 are **decimals**.
The dot '.' in a decimal is called a **decimal point**.

> Divide 1 whole into 10 equal parts.
> Each part is $\frac{1}{10}$ or 0.1.

1.

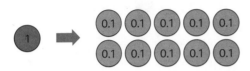

1 one   10 tenths

Write a decimal for each of the following:

(a)

0.1   0.1   0.1   0.1

4 tenths = ▇

(b)

0.1   0.1   0.1   0.1   0.1   0.1

6 tenths = ▇

(c)

0.1   0.1   0.1   0.1   0.1
0.1   0.1   0.1   0.1

9 tenths = ▇

2. Write each fraction as a decimal.

(a) 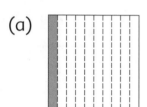   1 tenth

$$\frac{1}{10} = \blacksquare$$

(b) 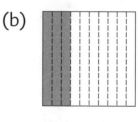   3 tenths

$$\frac{3}{10} = \blacksquare$$

(c) 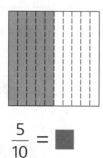   5 tenths

$$\frac{5}{10} = \blacksquare$$

(d) 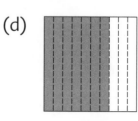   7 tenths

$$\frac{7}{10} = \blacksquare$$

3. Divide 1 m into 10 equal parts.
   Each part is 0.1 m.

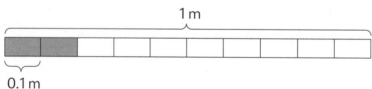

$$0.2 \text{ m} = \frac{2}{\blacksquare} \text{ of 1 m}$$

4. Divide 1 km into 10 equal parts.
   Each part is 0.1 km.

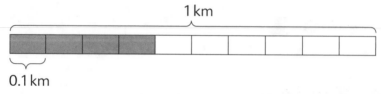

$$0.4 \text{ km} = \frac{\blacksquare}{10} \text{ of 1 km}$$

Workbook Exercise 1

5.

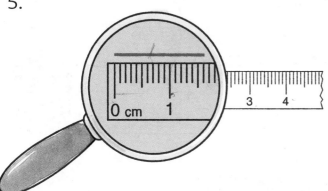

1.$\underline{6}$ = 1$\frac{6}{10}$

1.6 is also a decimal. We read 1.6 as **one point six**.

The length of the string is 1.6 cm.

(a)   1.6 cm is  cm longer than 1 cm.

(b)   1.6 = 1 + ▮

6.   (a)

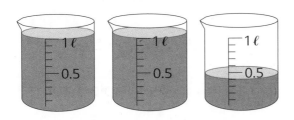

The total amount of water is ▮ ℓ.

(b)

The total weight of the cucumbers is ▮ kg.

Workbook Exercise 2

7. Write each fraction as a decimal.

(a)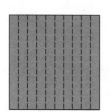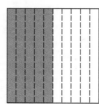

$1\frac{5}{10}$ =

$1\frac{5}{10} = 1 + \frac{5}{10}$

1 whole 5 tenths

(b)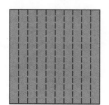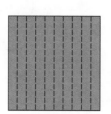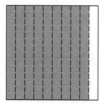

$2\frac{9}{10}$ = ■

2 wholes 9 tenths

8. Write the decimal represented by each letter.

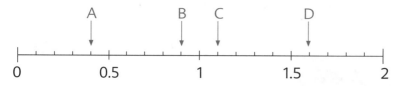

9. Write each decimal as a fraction in its simplest form.

(a) $0.2 = \frac{2}{10}$

= ■

(b) $1.2 = 1\frac{2}{10}$

= ■

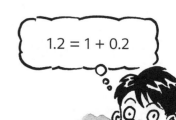

$1.2 = 1 + 0.2$

(c) $0.8 = $ ■

(d) $2.8 = $ ■

10. Which number is the smallest?

6.4, 5.8, 3.7, 9.1

11. Which number is the greatest?

2.7, 4.8, 8.5, 1.6

12. Arrange the numbers in increasing order.

(a) 3.1, 0.3, 3, 1.3

(b) 7.2, 2.7, 9, 7.8

Workbook Exercise 3

13. Write a decimal for each of the following:

(a)

2 ones   3 tenths

$2 + 0.3 = \blacksquare$

(b)
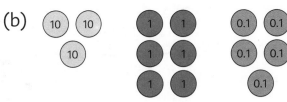

3 tens   6 ones   5 tenths

$30 + 6 + 0.5 = \blacksquare$

(c)
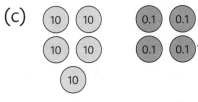

5 tens   4 tenths

$50 + 0.4 = \blacksquare$

14. Write a decimal for each of the following:

(a)
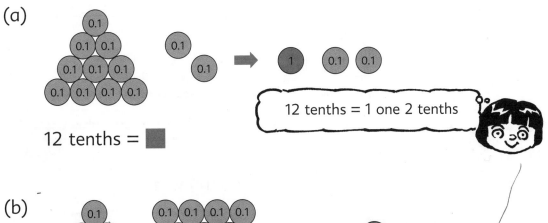

12 tenths = 1 one 2 tenths

12 tenths = $\blacksquare$

(b)
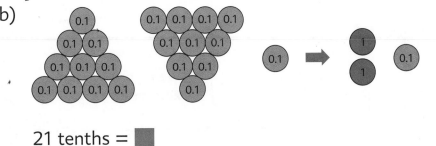

21 tenths = $\blacksquare$

Workbook Exercise 4

11

2 Hundredths

What is the length of the colored part?

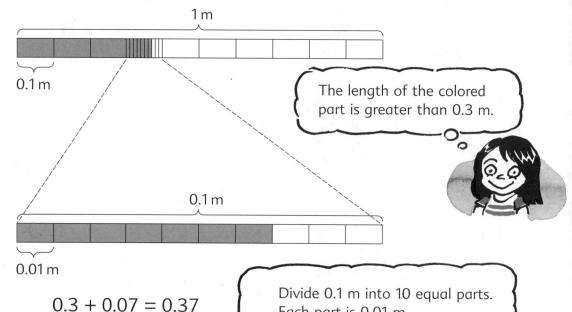

1 m

0.1 m

The length of the colored part is greater than 0.3 m.

0.1 m

0.01 m

$$0.3 + 0.07 = 0.37$$

Divide 0.1 m into 10 equal parts. Each part is 0.01 m.

The length of the colored part is 0.37 m.

0.01 is 1 hundredth.

$0.01 = \frac{1}{100}$

We read 0.01 as **zero point zero one**.

0.07 is 7 hundredths.

$0.07 = \frac{7}{100}$

We read 0.07 as **zero point zero seven**.

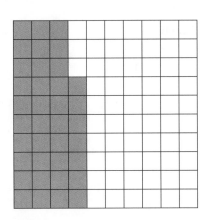

0.37 is 37 hundredths.

0.37 = $\frac{37}{100}$

We read 0.37 as **zero point three seven**.

0.37 is 3 tenths 7 hundredths.

0.37 = $\frac{3}{10}$ + $\frac{7}{100}$

1.

1 tenth   10 hundredths

Write a decimal for each of the following:

(a)

0.01 0.01 0.01

3 hundredths = ▨

(b)

0.01 0.01 0.01 0.01 0.01

5 hundredths = ▨

(c)

0.01 0.01 0.01 0.01 0.01   0.01 0.01

0.01 0.01 0.01 0.01 0.01

12 hundredths = ▨

2. Write a decimal for each of the following:

(a)

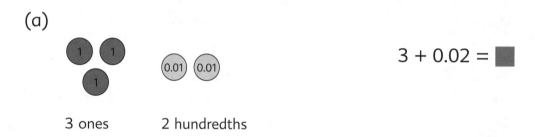

3 ones   2 hundredths

$3 + 0.02 = $ ∎

(b)

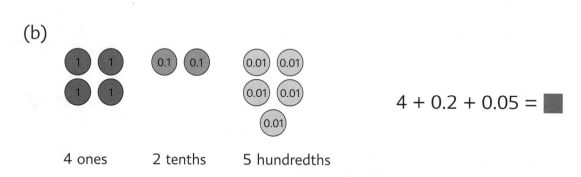

4 ones   2 tenths   5 hundredths

$4 + 0.2 + 0.05 = $ ∎

3.

Hundreds	Tens	Ones	Tenths	Hundredths
100 100	10 10 10	1 1 1 1	0.1 0.1 0.1 0.1 0.1	0.01 0.01 0.01 0.01 0.01 0.01

In 234.56, the digit 2 stands for 200.
What does each of the other digits stand for?

4.

Hundreds	Tens	Ones	Tenths	Hundredths
3	4	7	9	2

The number 347.92 has two decimal places.
The digit 9 is in the tenths place.
Its value is ∎.
The digit 2 is in the hundredths place.
Its value is ∎.
What is the value of each of the other digits?

The tenths place and the hundredths place are called **decimal places**.

Workbook Exercise 5

5. Write each fraction as a decimal.

(a)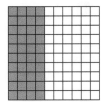

40 hundreths

$$\frac{40}{100} = \frac{4}{10}$$

$\frac{40}{100}$ = ▪

(b)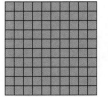

1 whole 28 hundredths

$1\frac{28}{100}$ = ▪

(c)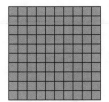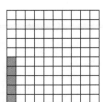

2 wholes 5 hundredths

$2\frac{5}{100}$ = ▪

6.

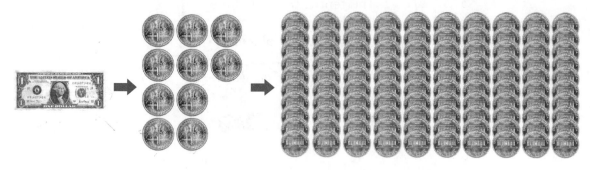

(a) $0.01 = 1¢

$0.01 is $\dfrac{\blacksquare}{100}$ of $1.

(b) $0.10 = 10¢

$0.10 is $\dfrac{\blacksquare}{10}$ of $1.

(c) $0.20 is $\dfrac{\blacksquare}{10}$ of $1.

$0.20 = $\blacksquare$ ¢

(d) 50¢ is $\dfrac{\blacksquare}{10}$ of $1.

50¢ = $\$\blacksquare$

(e) $0.45 is $\dfrac{\blacksquare}{100}$ of $1.

$0.45 = $\blacksquare$ ¢

(f) 26¢ is $\dfrac{\blacksquare}{100}$ of $1.

26¢ = $\$\blacksquare$

7. Write each of the following amount of money as a decimal.
   (a) 3 dollars 85 cents   (b) 6 dollars 50 cents
   (c) 8 dollars 5 cents   (d) 85 dollars

8. Find the value of
   (a) 2 + 0.84   (b) 30 + 6 + 0.25
   (c) 54 + 0.03   (d) 80 + 0.5 + 0.07

9. What number does each letter represent?

(a)

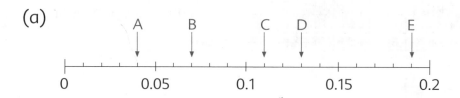

(b)

Workbook Exercise 6

10. (a) Express 0.25 as a fraction in its simplest form.

$$0.25 = \frac{25}{100}$$
$$= \blacksquare$$

(b) Express 1.84 as a fraction in its simplest form.

$$1.84 = 1\frac{84}{100}$$
$$= \blacksquare$$

11. Express each decimal as a fraction in its simplest form.
(a) 0.06   (b) 0.28   (c) 0.24
(d) 2.05   (e) 3.65   (f) 4.75

12. (a) Express $\frac{3}{5}$ as a decimal.

$$\frac{3}{5} = \frac{\blacksquare}{10}$$
$$= \blacksquare$$

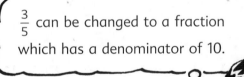

$\frac{3}{5}$ can be changed to a fraction which has a denominator of 10.

(b) Express $\frac{9}{20}$ as a decimal.

$$\frac{9}{20} = \frac{\blacksquare}{100}$$
$$= \blacksquare$$

$\frac{9}{20}$ can be changed to a fraction which has a denominator of 100.

13. Express each fraction as a decimal.

(a) $\frac{3}{4}$ (b) $\frac{7}{20}$ (c) $\frac{8}{25}$

(d) $1\frac{1}{2}$ (e) $2\frac{2}{5}$ (f) $3\frac{27}{50}$

Workbook Exercises 7 & 8

14. (a) Which is greater, 2.12 or 2.9?

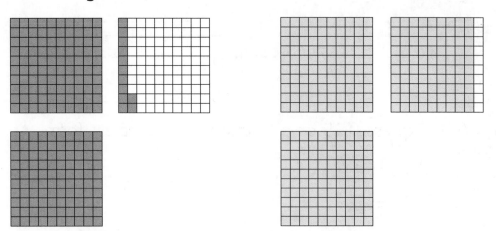

(b) Which is smaller, 1.68 or 2.35?

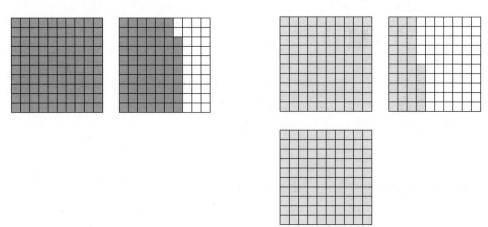

15. (a) Which is greater, 562.41 or 562.38?

Hundreds	Tens	Ones	Tenths	Hundredths
5	6	2	**4**	1
5	6	2	**3**	8

(b) Which is smaller, 89.67 or 243.5?

Hundreds	Tens	Ones	Tenths	Hundredths
	8	9	6	7
2	4	3	5	

16. (a) Which is greater, 42.6 or 42.06?
    (b) Which is longer, 2.38 m or 2.5 m?
    (c) Which is heavier, 32.6 kg or 3.26 kg?

17. Arrange the numbers in decreasing order.
    (a) 2.02, 0.2, 0.02, 2.2
    (b) 74.5, 7.45, 7.8, 80.7

Workbook Exercise 9

18. (a) What number is 0.1 more than 412.34?
    (b) What number is 0.1 less than 412.34?

19. (a) What number is 0.01 more than 123.48?
    (b) What number is 0.01 less than 123.48?

20. (a) Add 3 tenths to 4.87.
        The answer is ■.
    (b) Subtract 2 hundredths from 28.62.
        The answer is ■.

21. Find the value of
    (a) 86.43 + 0.2   (b) 24.8 + 0.05   (c) 4.87 + 0.02
    (d) 54.62 − 0.4   (e) 6.23 − 0.03   (f) 3.48 − 0.05

22. (a) 36.54 is ■ more than 36.
    (b) 36.54 is ■ more than 36.5.

23. What number must be added to 0.82 to give the answer 1?

82 + 18 = 100

Workbook Exercise 10

③ Thousandths

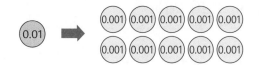

1 hundredth = 10 thousandths

Write a decimal for each of the following:

(a)

2 hundredths 4 thousandths =

(b)

3 tenths 1 hundredth 5 thousandths = ■

(c)

4 ones 2 thousandths = ■

1.

Tens	Ones	Tenths	Hundredths	Thousandths
10 10		0.1 0.1 0.1 0.1	0.01 0.01 0.01	0.001 0.001 0.001 0.001 0.001

20.435 has 3 **decimal places**.

(a) The digit 5 is in the thousandths place. What is its value?

(b) What is the value of each of the other digits?

The tenths place, hundredths place and thousandths place are called decimal places.

2. (a) What number is 0.01 more than 5.62?
   (b) What number is 0.01 less than 5.62?
   (c) What number is 0.001 more than 4.536?
   (d) What number is 0.001 less than 4.536?

3. What is the missing number in each ■?
   (a) 27.148 is ■ more than 27.
   (b) 27.148 is ■ more than 27.1.
   (c) 27.148 is ■ more than 27.14.

4. (a) Which is greater, 42.54 or 42.326?

Tens	Ones	Tenths	Hundredths	Thousandths
4	2	**5**	4	0
4	2	**3**	2	6

   (b) Which is smaller, 63.182 or 63.187?

Tens	Ones	Tenths	Hundredths	Thousandths
6	3	1	8	**2**
6	3	1	8	**7**

5. Arrange the numbers in decreasing order.
   (a) 0.320 0.302, 0.032, 3.02
   (b) 2.139, 2.628, 2.045, 2.189

6. Arrange the numbers in increasing order.
   (a) 5.8, 0.538, 0.830 3.58
   (b) 9.047, 9.076, 9.074, 9.067

Workbook Exercises 11 & 12

21

7. Express 0.052 as a fraction in its simplest form.

$$0.052 = \frac{52}{1000}$$

$$= \blacksquare$$

8. Express each decimal as a fraction in its simplest form.
    (a) 0.5
    (b) 0.08
    (c) 0.024
    (d) 0.345

9. Express 2.045 as a fraction in its simplest form.

$$2.045 = 2\frac{45}{1000}$$

$$= \blacksquare$$

10. Express each decimal as a fraction in its simplest form.
     (a) 2.6
     (b) 6.05
     (c) 3.002
     (d) 2.408

11. Arrange the numbers in increasing order.

     (a) $\frac{4}{5}$, 0.652, 2, 0.6

     (b) 7.231, $\frac{7}{25}$, $1\frac{3}{4}$, 0.35

Workbook Exercise 13

PRACTICE 1A

1. What is the value of the digit **6** in each of the following?
    (a) 1.**6**58   (b) **6**.185   (c) 3.0**6**9   (d) 5.74**6**

2. What is the missing number in each ■?
    (a) In 3.864, the digit ■ is in the thousandths place.
    (b) In 49.73, the digit ■ is in the tenths place.
    (c) In 12.5**8**, the value of the digit **8** is ■.
    (d) In 3.7**0**4, the value of the digit **4** is ■.

3. (a) What number is 0.1 less than 5.609?
    (b) What number is 0.01 more than 2.809?
    (c) What number is 0.001 less than 13.521?

4. Find the value of each of the following:
    (a) 0.7 + 0.02   (b) 3.7 + 0.08
    (c) 5.82 − 0.02   (d) 8.94 − 0.9

5. Express each decimal as a fraction in its simplest form.
    (a) 0.08   (b) 0.14   (c) 0.145   (d) 0.408
    (e) 3.6   (f) 1.12   (g) 4.506   (h) 2.006

6. Express each fraction as a decimal.

    (a) $\dfrac{9}{10}$ (b) $\dfrac{3}{100}$ (c) $\dfrac{39}{1000}$ (d) $\dfrac{105}{1000}$

    (e) $1\dfrac{7}{10}$ (f) $2\dfrac{18}{100}$ (g) $3\dfrac{7}{1000}$ (h) $\dfrac{999}{1000}$

7. What is the missing number in each ■?
    (a) 8.07 = 8 + ■   (b) 7.206 = 7 + ■ + 0.006
    (c) 12.96 = 10 + ■ + 0.9 + 0.06
    (d) 6.805 = 6 + 0.8 + ■

    (e) 5.012 = 5 + $\dfrac{1}{100}$ + $\dfrac{■}{1000}$ (f) 2.004 = 2 + $\dfrac{4}{■}$

23

PRACTICE 1B

1. Arrange the numbers in increasing order.
    (a) 0.008,   0.09,   0.08,   0.009
    (b) 3.25,   3.205,   3.025,   3.502
    (c) 4.386,   4.683,   4.638,   4.9
    (d) 10,   9.932,   9.392,   9.923

2. Express each fraction as a decimal.

    (a) $\dfrac{1}{2}$ (b) $\dfrac{3}{4}$ (c) $\dfrac{1}{5}$

    (d) $\dfrac{19}{5}$ (e) $6\dfrac{1}{4}$ (f) $4\dfrac{3}{5}$

3. Write **>** (is greater than), **<** (is less than) or **=** (is equal to) in each $\boxed{}$.

    (a) $\dfrac{47}{1000}$ $\boxed{}$ 0.047   (b) 0.205 $\boxed{}$ $\dfrac{25}{1000}$

    (c) $3\dfrac{3}{5}$ $\boxed{}$ 3.69   (d) 2.8 $\boxed{}$ $2\dfrac{4}{5}$

    (e) 1.425 $\boxed{}$ $1\dfrac{1}{4}$ (f) 0.87 $\boxed{}$ $\dfrac{78}{100}$

4. Write each of the following as a decimal.

    (a) $1 + \dfrac{7}{10} + \dfrac{3}{1000}$ (b) $\dfrac{8}{100} + \dfrac{5}{1000}$

    (c) $5 + \dfrac{6}{100} + \dfrac{9}{1000}$ (d) $10 + \dfrac{52}{1000}$

5. Find the value of each of the following:
    (a) 0.2 + 0.04 + 0.008   (b) 0.7 + 0.09 + 0.002
    (c) 3 + 0.7 + 0.08   (d) 10 + 0.5 + 0.004
    (e) 7 + 0.009   (f) 9 + 0.8 + 0.003

4 Rounding Off

The height of this hill is 164.3 m.

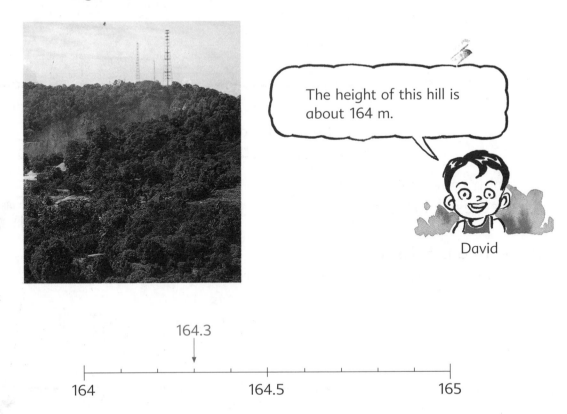

> The height of this hill is about 164 m.

David

164.3

164 ————— 164.5 ————— 165

David rounds off 164.3 to the nearest whole number.

> 164.3 is between 164 and 165.
> It is nearer to 164 than to 165.

David

164.3 is 164 when rounded off to the nearest whole number.

1. John weighs 37.4 kg.
   Round off his weight to the nearest kilogram.

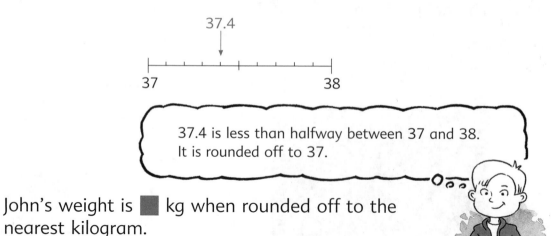

   37.4 is less than halfway between 37 and 38.
   It is rounded off to 37.

   John's weight is ■ kg when rounded off to the
   nearest kilogram.

2. A tree is 5.78 m tall.
   Round off its height to the nearest meter.

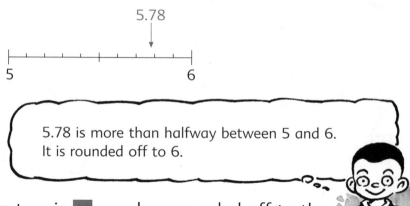

   5.78 is more than halfway between 5 and 6.
   It is rounded off to 6.

   The height of the tree is ■ m when rounded off to the
   nearest meter.

3. Round off 24.5 to the nearest whole number.

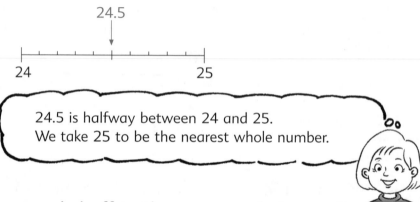

   24.5 is halfway between 24 and 25.
   We take 25 to be the nearest whole number.

   24.5 is ■ when rounded off to the nearest whole number.

4. Round off each of the following to the nearest whole number.
   (a) 4.2   (b) 13.9   (c) 29.5
   (d) 5.45   (e) 15.64   (f) 18.52

Workbook Exercise 14

5. The length of a string is 3.18 m.
   (a) Round off 3.18 m to the nearest meter.

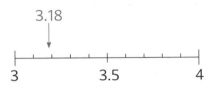 

   3.18 m is ▮ when rounded off to the nearest meter.

   (b) Round off 3.18 m to 1 decimal place.

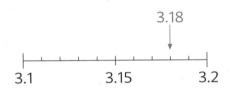 

   3.18 m is ▮ m when rounded off to 1 decimal place.

6.

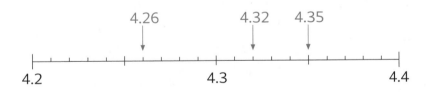

   (a) 4.26 is ▮ when rounded off to 1 decimal place.
   (b) 4.32 is ▮ when rounded off to 1 decimal place.
   (c) 4.35 is ▮ when rounded off to 1 decimal place.

7. Round off each of the following to 1 decimal place.
   (a) 0.91   (b) 2.45   (c) 7.08
   (d) 10.96   (e) 18.01   (f) 24.55

Workbook Exercise 15

REVIEW A

1. Write the missing number in each .
   (a) $57.42 = 57 + \blacksquare + 0.02$ (b) $9.62 = 9.6 + \blacksquare$

   (c) $2.53 = 2 + \dfrac{5}{10} + \dfrac{\blacksquare}{100}$ (d) $26.48 = 26 + \dfrac{48}{\blacksquare}$

2. Arrange the numbers in decreasing order.
   (a) 3.03, 0.3, 0.03, 3.3
   (b) 63.5, 6.35, 6.4, 5.63
   (c) 0.05, 0.29, 0.305, 0.009

3. Find the value of each of the following:
   (a) $30 + 0.06$ (b) $16.52 + 0.3$
   (c) $24.72 - 0.7$ (d) $73.26 - 0.06$

4. Round off each of the following to the nearest whole number.
   (a) 3.2   (b) 0.99   (c) 12.8
   (d) 10.09   (e) 3.95   (f) 4.55
   (g) 10.28   (h) 19.51

5. Round off each of the following to 1 decimal place.
   (a) 0.82   (b) 0.09   (c) 2.65
   (d) 8.07   (e) 10.89   (f) 19.07
   (g) 20.55   (h) 10.05

6. Round off each of the following to the nearest ten.
   (a) 589   (b) 2834   (c) 12,097

7. Round off each of the following to the nearest hundred.
   (a) 5650   (b) 13,845   (c) 45,090

8. (a) What number is 0.05 less than 4.1?
   (b) What number is 0.05 more than 4.1?

9. (a) Find the product of 13 and 469.
    (b) Find the quotient and remainder when 3278
         is divided by 9.

10. What is the missing number in each ■ ?
    (a) 45,700 = ■ + 40,000   (b) 35,000 = ■ × 3500
    (c) 91,548 = ■ + 1548   (d) 67,320 = 67,000 + ■

11. What fraction of each figure is shaded?
    Write the fractions in their simplest form.

    (a) 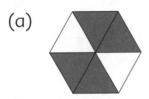   (b)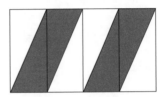

12. Add or subtract. Give each answer in its simplest form.

    (a) $\dfrac{8}{9} + \dfrac{8}{9}$ (b) $\dfrac{2}{3} + \dfrac{4}{9}$ (c) $\dfrac{5}{8} + \dfrac{3}{4}$

    (d) $4 - \dfrac{7}{10}$ (e) $5 - \dfrac{3}{10}$ (f) $6 - \dfrac{3}{4}$

13. Multiply. Give each answer in its simplest form.

    (a) $4 \times \dfrac{1}{4}$ (b) $\dfrac{1}{5} \times 5$ (c) $7 \times \dfrac{1}{2}$

    (d) $5 \times \dfrac{2}{3}$ (e) $\dfrac{3}{10} \times 8$ (f) $\dfrac{4}{9} \times 6$

14. Express each of the following as a decimal.

    (a) $4\dfrac{3}{100}$ (b) $1\dfrac{3}{5}$ (c) $10\dfrac{17}{20}$ (d) $5\dfrac{3}{4}$

15. Express each of the following as a fraction in its simplest form.
    (a) 0.8   (b) 1.25   (c) 4.45   (d) 6.06

16. Write a decimal in each .

(a)

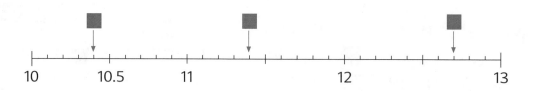

(b)

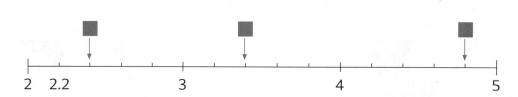

17. There are 215 pens and 5 times as many pencils in a box.
    (a) How many more pencils than pens are there?
    (b) What is the total number of pens and pencils?

18. Aly made 5 glasses of pineapple juice.

    If each glass contained $\frac{2}{5}$ liter of pineapple juice, how many liters of pineapple juice did Aly make altogether?

19. Kathy had $20.

    She used $\frac{3}{4}$ of the money to buy a book.
    How much money did she have left?

20. $\frac{4}{5}$ of 40 children can swim.
    How many children **cannot** swim?

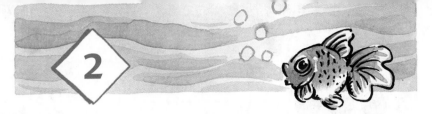

The Four Operations of Decimals

1 Addition and Subtraction

David drank 0.7 liter of milk.
John drank 0.2 liter of milk.

(a) How much milk did they drink altogether?

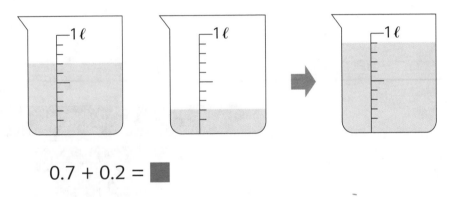

0.7 + 0.2 = ▮

They drank ▮ liter of milk altogether.

(b) How much more milk did David drink than John?

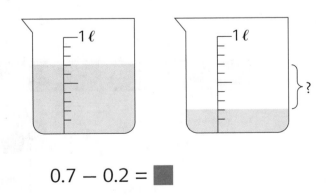

0.7 − 0.2 = ▮

David drank ▮ liter more milk than John.

1. (a) Add 0.4 and 0.3.

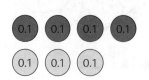

4 tenths + 3 tenths
= 7 tenths

0.4 + 0.3 = ■

(b) Add 0.04 and 0.03.

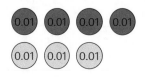

4 hundredths + 3 hundredths
= 7 hundredths

0.04 + 0.03 = ■

2. Add 0.7 and 0.6.

$$
\begin{array}{r}
0.7 \\
+\ 0.6 \\
\hline
1.3
\end{array}
$$

Ones	Tenths	Hundredths
1	0.1 0.1 0.1 0.1 0.1 0.1 0.1 0.1 0.1 0.1 0.1 0.1 0.1	

3. Add 0.07 and 0.06.

$$
\begin{array}{r}
0.07 \\
+\ 0.06 \\
\hline
0.13
\end{array}
$$

Ones	Tenths	Hundredths
	0.1	0.01 0.01 0.01 0.01 0.01 0.01 0.01 0.01 0.01 0.01 0.01 0.01 0.01

4. Find the value of
   (a) 0.6 + 0.2   (b) 0.8 + 0.5   (c) 0.3 + 0.9
   (d) 0.02 + 0.04   (e) 0.07 + 0.03   (f) 0.08 + 0.09

Workbook Exercise 16

5. Add 6.9 and 0.4.

   6.9 + 0.4 = 6 + 1.3
            = ■

6.9 + 0.4
6   0.9
0.9 + 0.4 = 1.3

6. Add 3.6 and 1.8.

      3 . 6
   + 1 . 8
      ■

Ones	Tenths	Hundredths

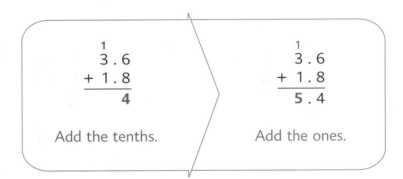

$$\begin{array}{r} 1 \\ 3\,.\,6 \\ +\ 1\,.\,8 \\ \hline 4 \end{array}$$

Add the tenths.

$$\begin{array}{r} 1 \\ 3\,.\,6 \\ +\ 1\,.\,8 \\ \hline 5\,.\,4 \end{array}$$

Add the ones.

7. Find the value of
   (a) 8 + 0.5   (b) 2.8 + 0.7   (c) 3.4 + 0.6
   (d) 2.6 + 7   (e) 3.7 + 2.3   (f) 4.9 + 1.8

Workbook Exercise 17

8. (a) Add 0.42 and 0.9.

$$0.42 + 0.9 = 0.02 + 1.3$$
$$= \blacksquare$$

0.42 + 0.9

0.4   0.02

0.4 + 0.9 = 1.3

(b) Add 0.42 and 0.09.

$$0.42 + 0.09 = 0.4 + 0.11$$
$$= \blacksquare$$

0.42 + 0.09

0.4   0.02

0.02 + 0.09 = 0.11

9. Add 0.24 and 0.37.

```
   0 . 2 4
 + 0 . 3 7
 ━━━━━━━━━
```

Ones	Tenths	Hundredths
	0.1 0.1 (0.1)	0.01 0.01 0.01 0.01
	0.1 0.1 0.1	0.01 0.01 0.01 0.01 0.01 0.01 0.01

```
      1
   0 . 2 4
 + 0 . 3 7
 ━━━━━━━━━
         1
```
Add the hundredths.

```
      1
   0 . 2 4
 + 0 . 3 7
 ━━━━━━━━━
   0 . 6 1
```
Add the tenths.

10. Find the value of
   (a) 0.63 + 2   (b) 0.56 + 0.4   (c) 0.84 + 0.3
   (d) 6 + 0.02   (e) 0.37 + 0.03   (f) 0.97 + 0.06
   (g) 4 + 0.28   (h) 0.65 + 0.53   (i) 0.86 + 0.49
   (j) 1.49 + 6   (k) 2.46 + 0.6   (l) 3.94 + 0.06

11. Add 2.63 and 3.84.

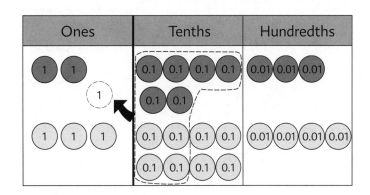

```
  2 . 6 3
+ 3 . 8 4
```

2 . 6 3 + 3 . 8 4 ———— **7**	¹ 2 . 6 3 + 3 . 8 4 ———— **4** 7	¹ 2 . 6 3 + 3 . 8 4 ———— **6** . 4 7
Add the hundredths.	Add the tenths.	Add the ones.

12. Add.
    (a) 25.48 + 7.64 = ▣   (b) 4.8 + 2.37 = ▣

```
      2 5 . 4 8
    +     7 . 6 4
```

```
      4 . 8 0
    + 2 . 3 7
```

13. Estimate the value of 34.26 + 10.82.

34 + 11 = 45

14. Estimate and then add.
    (a) 2.96 + 6.8   (b) 3.64 + 2.7   (c) 3.2 + 3.98
    (d) 3.54 + 2.38   (e) 6.57 + 2.86   (f) 8.92 + 4.16

Workbook Exercises 18 & 19

15. (a) Subtract 0.2 from 0.8.

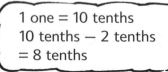

8 tenths — 2 tenths
= 6 tenths

$0.8 - 0.2 = $ ■

(b) Subtract 0.2 from 1.

1 one = 10 tenths
10 tenths — 2 tenths
= 8 tenths

$1 - 0.2 = $ ■

(c) Subtract 0.2 from 3.

$3 - 0.2 = $ ■

16. Subtract 0.8 from 4.2.

$$\begin{array}{r} \overset{3}{\cancel{4}} . \overset{12}{\cancel{2}} \\ -\ 0\ .\ 8 \\ \hline 3\ .\ 4 \end{array}$$

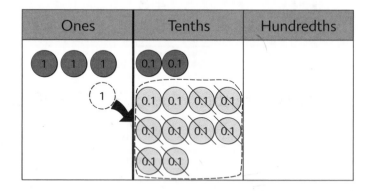

Ones	Tenths	Hundredths

17. Find the value of
    (a) $0.5 - 0.3$ (b) $0.7 - 0.5$ (c) $0.9 - 0.2$
    (d) $1 - 0.4$ (e) $2 - 0.7$ (f) $4 - 0.9$
    (g) $1.4 - 0.8$ (h) $4.7 - 0.6$ (i) $5.3 - 0.9$
    (j) $0.58 - 0.3$ (k) $4.05 - 0.5$ (l) $5.12 - 0.4$

Workbook Exercise 20

18. (a) Subtract 0.06 from 0.08.

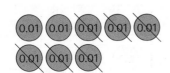

8 hundredths — 6 hundredths = 2 hundredths

$0.08 - 0.06 =$ ◼

(b) Subtract 0.06 from 0.1.

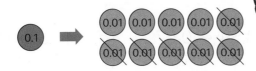

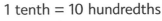

1 tenth = 10 hundredths

$0.1 - 0.06 =$ ◼

(c) Subtract 0.06 from 1.

$1 - 0.06 =$ ◼

1 one = 9 tenths 10 hundredths

19. Subtract 0.23 from 1.

$1 - 0.23 =$ ◼

20. Find the value of
(a) $0.09 - 0.02$ (b) $0.49 - 0.02$ (c) $3.49 - 0.02$
(d) $0.1 - 0.04$ (e) $0.3 - 0.04$ (f) $2.3 - 0.04$
(g) $1 - 0.07$ (h) $2 - 0.07$ (i) $4 - 0.09$
(j) $1 - 0.45$ (k) $3 - 0.45$ (l) $4 - 0.86$

21. Subtract 0.08 from 4.2.

$$
\begin{array}{r}
\overset{\overset{1\ \ 10}{}}{4\,.\,\cancel{2}\,\cancel{0}} \\
-\ 0\,.\,0\,8 \\
\hline
4\,.\,1\,2
\end{array}
$$

Ones	Tenths	Hundredths
1 1 1 1	0.1 (0.1)	0.01 0.01 0.01 0.01 / 0.01 0.01 0.01 0.01 / 0.01 0.01

22. Find the value of
    (a) 3.29 − 0.06   (b) 3.54 − 0.07   (c) 4.25 − 0.09
    (d) 4.8 − 0.06   (e) 6.2 − 0.07   (f) 6.5 − 0.09

Workbook Exercise 21

23. Subtract 2.7 from 6.

$$
\begin{array}{r}
\overset{\overset{5\ \ 10}{}}{\cancel{6}\,.\,\cancel{0}} \\
-\ 2\,.\,7 \\
\hline

\end{array}
$$

Ones	Tenths	Hundredths
1 1 1 1 / 1 1	0.1 0.1 0.1 0.1 / 0.1 0.1 0.1 0.1 / 0.1 0.1	

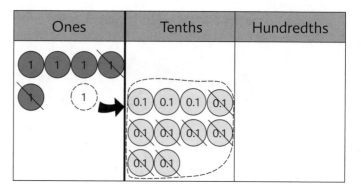

$$
\begin{array}{r}
\overset{\overset{5\ \ 10}{}}{\cancel{6}\,.\,\cancel{0}} \\
-\ 2\,.\,7 \\
\hline
3
\end{array}
$$

Subtract the tenths.

$$
\begin{array}{r}
\overset{\overset{5\ \ 10}{}}{\cancel{6}\,.\,\cancel{0}} \\
-\ 2\,.\,7 \\
\hline
3\,.\,3
\end{array}
$$

Subtract the ones.

24. Find the value of
    (a) 4.9 − 1.3   (b) 5.2 − 1.7   (c) 5.5 − 2.8
    (d) 4.1 − 1.6   (e) 5 − 2.4   (f) 8 − 3.2

Workbook Exercise 22

25. Subtract 2.53 from 4.27.

$$
\begin{array}{r}
4.27 \\
- 2.53 \\
\hline
\end{array}
$$

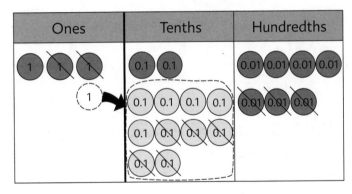

	4.27 − 2.53 —— **4**	3 12 4.$\cancel{2}$7 − 2.53 —— **7**4	3 12 4.$\cancel{2}$7 − 2.53 —— **1**.**7**4
	Subtract the hundredths.	Subtract the tenths.	Subtract the ones.

26. Subtract.
   (a) 7.24 − 3.5 = ■

$$
\begin{array}{r}
7.24 \\
- 3.50 \\
\hline
\end{array}
$$

   (b) 0.8 − 0.49 = ■

$$
\begin{array}{r}
0.80 \\
- 0.49 \\
\hline
\end{array}
$$

   (c) 5 − 1.27 = ■

$$
\begin{array}{r}
5.00 \\
- 1.27 \\
\hline
\end{array}
$$

   (d) 6.2 − 3.54 = ■

$$
\begin{array}{r}
6.20 \\
- 3.54 \\
\hline
\end{array}
$$

27. Find the value of
   (a) 0.85 − 0.43   (b) 0.64 − 0.39   (c) 1.54 − 0.66
   (d) 4.72 − 1.32   (e) 5.87 − 2.38   (f) 6.05 − 2.5
   (g) 0.6 − 0.16   (h) 2.9 − 0.75   (i) 2.1 − 0.48
   (j) 3.4 − 1.85   (k) 6 − 2.56   (l) 4.5 − 3.55

Workbook Exercises 23 & 24

28. Estimate the value of 27.82 − 8.3.

28 − 8 = 20

29. Estimate and then add.
    (a) 8.67 + 7.2   (b) 42.36 + 7.65   (c) 20.81 + 18.76

30. Estimate and then subtract.
    (a) 7.23 − 4.6   (b) 30.45 − 8.56   (c) 52.36 − 24.82

31. Add 4.28 and 2.99.

    4.28 + 2.99 = 7.28 − 0.01
                = ▮

4.28 + 3 = 7.28

32. Add 8.99 and 0.99.

    8.99 + 0.99 = 10 − 0.02
                = ▮

9 + 1 = 10

33. Subtract 1.99 from 5.62.

    5.62 − 1.99 = 3.62 + 0.01
                = ▮

5.62 − 2 = 3.62

34. Find the value of
    (a) 3.87 + 1.99   (b) 2.99 + 7.81   (c) 3.99 + 5.99
    (d) 4.52 − 0.99   (e) 5.03 − 2.99   (f) 8.1 − 3.99

Workbook Exercise 25

35. At a store, Mrs. Lee paid $1.75 for a pen,
$3.99 for a pair of slippers and $5.40 for a book.
How much did she spend altogether?

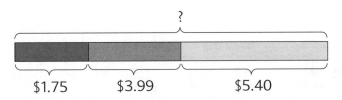

$1.75 $3.99 $5.40

$1.75 + $3.99 + $5.40 = ▮

She spent $▮ altogether.

36. Emily has a white ribbon and a blue ribbon.
The white ribbon is 1.85 m long.
The blue ribbon is 1.4 m longer than the white ribbon.
Find the total length of the two ribbons.

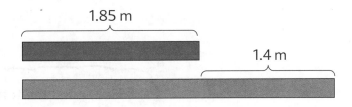

1.85 + 1.4 = 3.25

First, I find the length of
the blue ribbon.

The length of the blue ribbon is 3.25 m.

1.85 + 3.25 = ▮

The total length is ▮ m.

37. Samantha bought a fish for $5.25.
She also bought some shrimps for $11.80.
She paid with a $50 bill.
How much change did she receive?

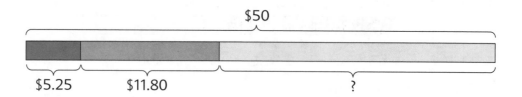

$50

$5.25 $11.80   ?

Method 1:

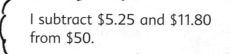

I subtract $5.25 and $11.80 from $50.

$50 − $5.25 − $11.80 = $▨

She received $▨ change.

Method 2:

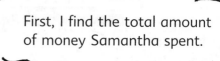

First, I find the total amount of money Samantha spent.

$5.25 + $11.80 = $17.05

She spent $17.05 altogether.

$50 − $17.05 = $▨

She received $▨ change.

Workbook Exercises 26 & 27

PRACTICE 2A

Find the value of each of the following:

	(a)	(b)	(c)
1.	0.5 + 0.4	0.8 + 0.9	3.2 + 0.9
2.	0.02 + 0.08	0.07 + 0.04	0.76 + 0.5
3.	0.9 − 0.8	2 − 0.4	3.2 − 0.6
4.	0.06 − 0.03	1 − 0.07	4 − 0.65
5.	4.7 + 3.6	0.58 + 0.24	0.82 + 1.2
6.	6.8 − 4.3	0.92 − 0.08	1.46 − 0.59

7. Round off the numbers to the nearest whole number and then find the value of each of the following:
   (a) 2.56 + 6.29   (b) 1.08 + 6.5   (c) 16.39 + 3.65
   (d) 3.56 − 0.76   (e) 9.31 − 4.8   (f) 5.62 − 1.98

8. Tracy is 1.32 m tall.
   She is 0.07 m taller than Brianne.
   How tall is Brianne?

9. Samantha spent $5.75 on vegetables.
   She spent $7.50 more on meat than on vegetables.
   How much did she spend on meat?

10. After spending $3.60, Pablo had $16.80 left.
    How much money did he have at first?

11. Nathan's weight was 42.5 kg three years ago.
    Now he weighs 38.6 kg.
    How much weight did he lose?

12. Fred's time in a race was 14.5 seconds.
    Jordan's time was 15.3 seconds.
    Who ran faster and how much faster?

PRACTICE 2B

Find the value of each of the following:

	(a)	(b)	(c)
1.	40.23 + 8.45	18.06 + 1.37	26.29 + 13.73
2.	24.9 + 3.7	10.99 + 6.32	12.99 + 6.99
3.	13.58 − 0.25	24.5 − 2.27	17.02 − 12.13
4.	39.45 − 2.8	16.04 − 4.99	25.6 − 14.99

5. A pineapple weighs 1.69 lb.
   A watermelon is 2.51 lb heavier than the pineapple.
   What is the total weight of the two fruits?

6. Kate bought 3 liters of milk.
   She drank 0.5 liter and used 0.25 liter to make cookies.
   How many liters of milk did she have left?

7. Mitchell jogged 5.85 km on Saturday.
   He jogged 1.7 km less on Sunday than on Saturday.
   What was the total distance he jogged on the two days?

8. After using 24.8 cm of ribbon to tie a present and 12.6 cm to
   make a bow, Annie had 18.4 cm of ribbon left.
   How many centimeters of ribbon did she have at first?

9. Morgan, Annie and Lucy went shopping and spent a total
   of $15.
   Morgan spent $4.15 and Annie spent $6.80.
   How much did Lucy spend?

10. Mrs. Bates bought a bottle of apple juice for $4.90 and 1 kg
    of grapes for $7.50.
    She gave the cashier $15.
    How much change did she receive?

② Multiplication

Jean drinks 0.4 liter of milk a day.
How many liters of milk does she drink in 3 days?

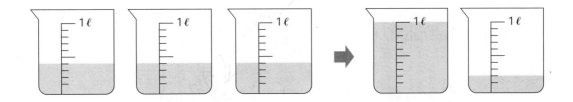

$0.4 \times 3 = \blacksquare$

She drinks $\blacksquare$ liters of milk in 3 days.

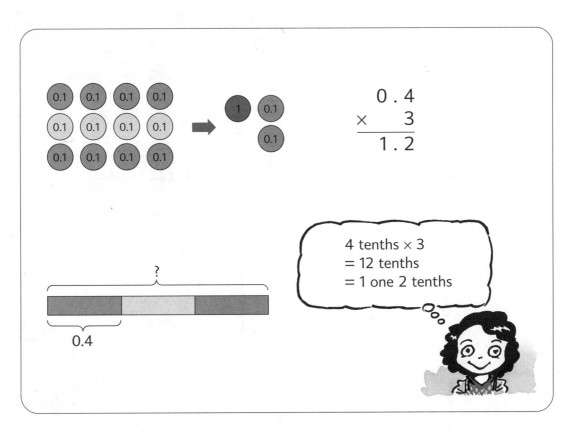

$$\begin{array}{r} 0.4 \\ \times \quad 3 \\ \hline 1.2 \end{array}$$

4 tenths × 3
= 12 tenths
= 1 one 2 tenths

1. (a) Multiply 0.2 by 4.

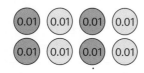

$0.2 \times 4 = \blacksquare$

2 tenths × 4
= 8 tenths

(b) Multiply 0.02 by 4.

$0.02 \times 4 = \blacksquare$

2 hundredths × 4
= 8 hundredths

2. (a) Multiply 0.7 by 3.

$0.7 \times 3 = \blacksquare$

$$
\begin{array}{r}
0\,.\,7 \\
\times \quad 3 \\
\hline
2\,.\,1 \\
\end{array}
$$

Ones	Tenths	Hundredths

(b) Multiply 0.6 by 5.

$0.6 \times 5 = \blacksquare$

6 tenths × 5
= 30 tenths
= 3 ones

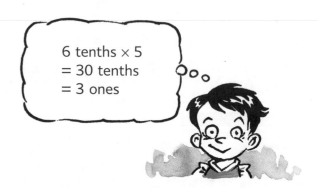

3. (a) Multiply 0.07 by 3.

$0.07 \times 3 = $ ■

Ones	Tenths	Hundredths

$$\begin{array}{r} 0.07 \\ \times \quad 3 \\ \hline 0.21 \end{array}$$

(b) Multiply 0.06 by 5.

$0.06 \times 5 = $ ■

6 hundredths × 5
= 30 hundredths
= 3 tenths

4. Find the value of
   (a) 3×2 (b) 0.3×2 (c) 0.03×2
   (d) 4×7 (e) 0.4×7 (f) 0.04×7
   (g) 5×8 (h) 0.5×8 (i) 0.05×8

5. Multiply $0.80 by 4.

$\$0.80 \times 4 = \$$ ■

$$\begin{array}{r} \$0.80 \\ \times \quad 4 \\ \hline \$3.20 \end{array}$$

6. Find the value of
   (a) $\$0.20 \times 4$ (b) $\$0.60 \times 7$ (c) $\$0.90 \times 8$

Workbook Exercise 28

7. Multiply 0.25 by 3.

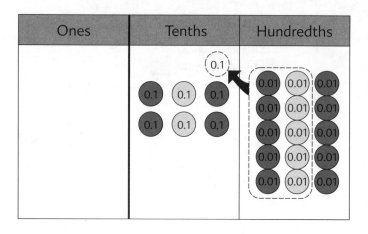

$$
\begin{array}{r}
0\,.\,2\,5 \\
\times \qquad 3 \\
\hline
\end{array}
$$

$$
\begin{array}{r}
\overset{1}{}\,.\,2\,5 \\
0\,.\,2\,5 \\
\times \qquad 3 \\
\hline
5
\end{array}
$$

Multiply 5 hundredths by 3.

$$
\begin{array}{r}
\overset{1}{}.\,2\,5 \\
0\,.\,2\,5 \\
\times \qquad 3 \\
\hline
\mathbf{0}\,.\,\mathbf{7}\,5
\end{array}
$$

Multiply 2 tenths by 3.

8. Multiply 4.53 by 2.

$$
\begin{array}{r}
4\,.\,5\,3 \\
\times \qquad 2 \\
\hline
\end{array}
$$

| Ones | Tenths | Hundredths |

$$
\begin{array}{r}
4\,.\,5\,3 \\
\times \qquad 2 \\
\hline
6
\end{array}
$$

Multiply 3 hundredths by 2.

$$
\begin{array}{r}
\overset{1}{4}\,.\,5\,3 \\
\times \qquad 2 \\
\hline
\mathbf{0}\,6
\end{array}
$$

Multiply 5 tenths by 2.

$$
\begin{array}{r}
\overset{1}{4}\,.\,5\,3 \\
\times \qquad 2 \\
\hline
\mathbf{9}\,.\,0\,6
\end{array}
$$

Multiply 4 ones by 2.

9. Find the value of
   (a) 4.3 × 3   (b) 0.26 × 4   (c) 3.12 × 4
   (d) 5.9 × 2   (e) 0.45 × 5   (f) 4.52 × 8

10. Multiply.
   (a) 20.7 × 6 = ■   (b) 8 × 32.6 = ■

```
      2 0 . 7                              3 2 . 6
   ×        6                           ×        8
   ───────────                          ───────────
   ███████████                          ███████████
```

   (c) 46.01 × 9 = ■   (d) 7 × 25.83 = ■

```
      4 6 . 0 1                            2 5 . 8 3
   ×          9                         ×          7
   ─────────────                        ─────────────
   █████████████                        █████████████
```

11. Find the value of
   (a) 18.5 × 2   (b) 34.02 × 3   (c) 48.26 × 6
   (d) 3 × 26.8   (e) 5 × 36.15   (f) 8 × 55.25

12. Estimate the value of 6.84 × 9.

7 × 9 = 63

13. Estimate and then multiply.
   (a) 3.9 × 5   (b) 0.72 × 8   (c) 29.73 × 6

14. Find the value of
   (a) $2.05 × 4   (b) $19.50 × 6   (c) $32.45 × 9

Workbook Exercises 29 to 31

15. Jared sold 6 books at $3.95 each.
    How much money did he collect altogether?

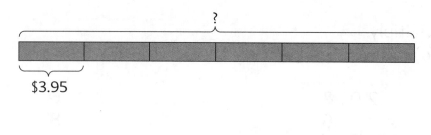

$$\$3.95 \times 6 = \$\blacksquare$$

He collected $\blacksquare altogether.

16. Rachel saved $20.05.
    Susan saved 4 times as much as Rachel.
    How much did Susan save?

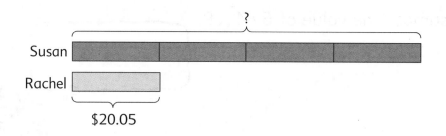

$$\$20.05 \times 4 = \$\blacksquare$$

Susan saved $\blacksquare.

Workbook Exercise 32

17. Sam had $30.
He bought 4 sets of stamps from a post office.
Each set of stamps cost $2.95.
How much money did he have left?

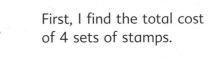
First, I find the total cost
of 4 sets of stamps.

$2.95 × 4 = $11.80

4 sets of stamps cost $11.80.

$30 − $11.80 = $■

He had $■ left.

18. Sophie bought some material to make 6 curtains.
She used 3.15 m for each curtain.
She had 2.5 m of material left after making the curtains.
How many meters of material did she buy?

3.15 × 6 = 18.9

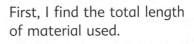
First, I find the total length
of material used.

She used 18.9 m of material.

18.9 + 2.5 = ■

She bought ■ m of material.

Workbook Exercise 33

PRACTICE 2C

Find the value of each of the following:

	(a)	(b)	(c)
1.	2.5 + 6.1	4.2 + 6.8	1.38 + 0.9
2.	2.7 + 3.53	2.45 + 2.07	3.18 + 0.96
3.	7.8 − 2.5	8.2 − 4.7	4.6 − 2.75
4.	5 − 3.48	9.05 − 5.88	7.21 − 4.36
5.	0.4 × 9	7 × 0.8	0.31 × 6
6.	3 × 0.45	1.5 × 4	3.86 × 5

7. Estimate and then multiply.
   (a) 3.2 × 6   (b) 2.48 × 3   (c) 4.09 × 5

8. In a high jump event, Cameron cleared 1.5 m and Jordan cleared 1.39 m.
   Find the difference between the two results.

9. A worker mixed 13.45 lb of cement with sand.
   The weight of sand used was 3 times the weight of the cement.
   How many pounds of sand did he use?

10. Mrs. Lee bought 4 packets of spices and a can of cocoa.
    Each packet of spices cost $0.85 and the can of cocoa cost $3.75.
    How much did she spend altogether?

11. A painter mixed 1.46 liters of black paint with 0.8 liter of white paint to get gray paint.
    Then he used 0.96 liter of the gray paint.
    How much gray paint did he have left?

12. Mrs. Bates bought 5 pots of plant.
    Each pot of plant cost $2.35.
    She gave the cashier $20.
    How much change did she receive?

③ Division

Barry poured 0.9 liter of water equally into 3 beakers.
How much water was there in each beaker?

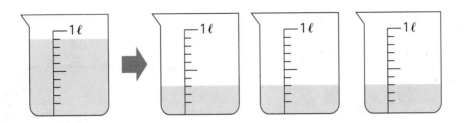

0.9 ÷ 3 = ■

There was ■ liter of water in each beaker.

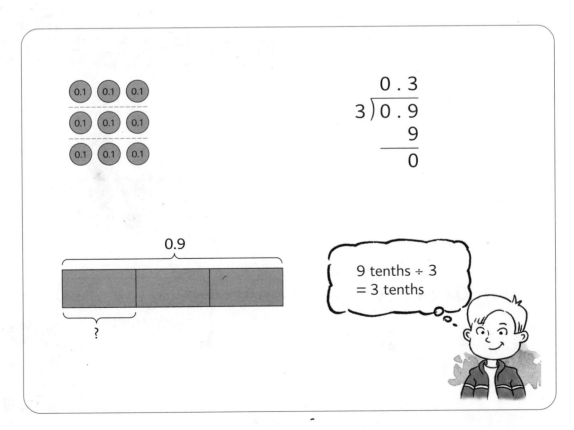

$$\begin{array}{r} 0.3 \\ 3\overline{)0.9} \\ 9 \\ \hline 0 \end{array}$$

9 tenths ÷ 3
= 3 tenths

1. (a) Divide 0.6 by 2.

$0.6 \div 2 = $ ■

6 tenths ÷ 2
= 3 tenths

(b) Divide 0.06 by 2.

$0.06 \div 2 = $ ■

6 hundredths ÷ 2
= 3 hundredths

2. (a) Divide 1.8 by 3.

$1.8 \div 3 = $ ■

18 tenths ÷ 3
= 6 tenths

$$\begin{array}{r} 0\,.\,6 \\ 3\overline{)1\,.\,8} \\ 1\,.\,8 \\ \hline 0 \end{array}$$

Ones	Tenths			Hundredths

(b) Divide 2 by 4.

$2 \div 4 = $ ■

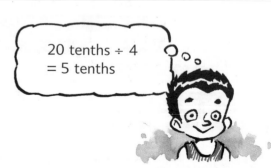

20 tenths ÷ 4
= 5 tenths

54

3. (a) Divide 0.18 by 3.

$0.18 \div 3 = \blacksquare$

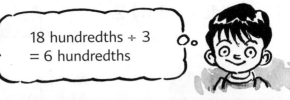

18 hundredths ÷ 3
= 6 hundredths

```
    0 . 0 6
3 ) 0 . 1 8
    1 8
    ─────
        0
```

Ones	Tenths	Hundredths

(b) Divide 0.2 by 4.

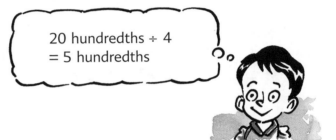

20 hundredths ÷ 4
= 5 hundredths

$0.2 \div 4 = \blacksquare$

4. Find the value of
   (a) $8 \div 4$ (b) $0.8 \div 4$ (c) $0.08 \div 4$
   (d) $35 \div 7$ (e) $3.5 \div 7$ (f) $0.35 \div 7$
   (g) $30 \div 5$ (h) $3 \div 5$ (i) $0.3 \div 5$

5. Divide $4.20 by 6.

$\$4.20 \div 6 = \$\blacksquare$

```
       $ 0 . 7 0
6 ) $ 4 . 2 0
    4  2
    ──────
          0
```

6. Find the value of
   (a) $\$0.90 \div 3$ (b) $\$2.40 \div 8$ (c) $\$5.40 \div 9$

Workbook Exercise 34

7. Divide 0.74 by 2.

$2\overline{)0.74}$

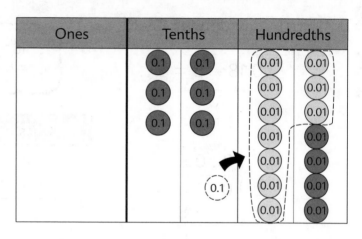

| Ones | Tenths | Hundredths |

Divide 7 tenths by 2.

$$\begin{array}{r} 0.3 \\ 2\overline{)0.74} \\ 6 \\ \hline 1 \end{array}$$

Divide 14 hundredths by 2.

$$\begin{array}{r} 0.37 \\ 2\overline{)0.74} \\ 6 \\ \hline 14 \\ 14 \\ \hline 0 \end{array}$$

8. Find the value of
   (a) 0.39 ÷ 3   (b) 0.84 ÷ 4   (c) 0.77 ÷ 7
   (d) 0.68 ÷ 4   (e) 0.75 ÷ 5   (f) 0.96 ÷ 6

9. Divide $0.60 by 4.

   $0.60 ÷ 4 = $■

$$\begin{array}{r} \$0.15 \\ 4\overline{)\$0.60} \\ 4 \\ \hline 20 \\ 20 \\ \hline 0 \end{array}$$

10. Find the value of
    (a) $0.30 ÷ 2   (b) $0.45 ÷ 3   (c) $0.95 ÷ 5
    (d) $3.55 ÷ 5   (e) $4.32 ÷ 6   (f) $5.04 ÷ 9

Workbook Exercise 35

11. Divide 4.35 by 3.

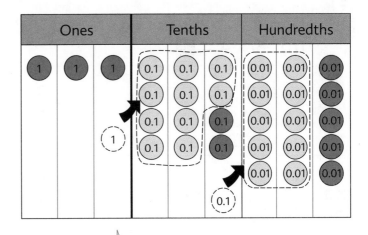

| | Ones | Tenths | Hundredths |

Divide 4 ones by 3.

$$\begin{array}{r} 1 \\ 3\overline{)4.35} \\ \underline{3} \\ 1 \end{array}$$

Divide 13 tenths by 3.

$$\begin{array}{r} 1.4 \\ 3\overline{)4.35} \\ \underline{3} \\ 1\ 3 \\ \underline{1\ 2} \\ 1 \end{array}$$

Divide 15 hundredths by 3.

$$\begin{array}{r} 1.45 \\ 3\overline{)4.35} \\ \underline{3} \\ 1\ 3 \\ \underline{1\ 2} \\ 1\ 5 \\ \underline{1\ 5} \\ 0 \end{array}$$

12. Find the value of
    (a) 3.96 ÷ 3   (b) 4.12 ÷ 4   (c) 14.58 ÷ 6

13. Divide $18.40 by 8.

    $18.40 ÷ 8 = $▇

$$\begin{array}{r} \$\ 2.30 \\ 8\overline{)\$18.40} \\ \underline{16} \\ 2\ 4 \\ \underline{2\ 4} \\ 0 \end{array}$$

14. Find the value of
    (a) $4.65 ÷ 3   (b) $16.50 ÷ 6   (c) $31.05 ÷ 9

Workbook Exercise 36

15. Divide.
(a) $5 \div 4 =$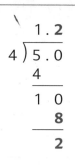

```
      1
   4 ) 5
      4
      1
```
Divide 5 ones
by 4.

```
      1 . 2
   4 ) 5 . 0
      4
      1 0
        8
        2
```
Divide 10 tenths
by 4.

```
      1 . 2 5
   4 ) 5 . 0 0
      4
      1 0
        8
        2 0
        2 0
          0
```
Divide 20 hundredths
by 4.

(b) $8.1 \div 6 =$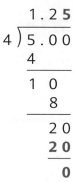

```
      1
   6 ) 8 . 1
      6
      2
```
Divide 8 ones
by 6.

```
      1 . 3
   6 ) 8 . 1
      6
      2 1
      1 8
        3
```
Divide 21 tenths
by 6.

```
      1 . 3 5
   6 ) 8 . 1 0
      6
      2 1
      1 8
        3 0
        3 0
          0
```
Divide 30 hundredths
by 6.

16. Divide.
(a) $30.4 \div 5 =$ ▆

(b) $12 \div 8 =$ ▆

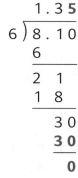

```
        ▆▆▆▆▆
   5 ) 3 0 . 4 0
```

```
        ▆▆▆▆
   8 ) 1 2 . 0
```

17. Find the value of
(a) $8 \div 5$
(b) $15 \div 6$
(c) $22 \div 8$
(d) $0.9 \div 2$
(e) $1.7 \div 5$
(f) $25.5 \div 6$

Workbook Exercise 37

18. Estimate the value of $31.2 \div 8$.

$32 \div 8 = 4$

19. Estimate the value of $5.28 \div 6$.

$5.4 \div 6 = 0.9$

20. Estimate and then divide.
   (a) $0.81 \div 3$ (b) $7.12 \div 8$ (c) $46.35 \div 9$

21. Find the value of $7 \div 3$ correct to 1 decimal place.

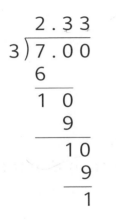

```
       2 . 3 3
   3 ) 7 . 0 0
       6
       ─────
       1 0
         9
       ─────
         1 0
           9
         ─────
           1
```

Divide to 2 decimal places.
Then round off the answer
to 1 decimal place.

2.33 is ■ when rounded off to 1 decimal place.

$7 \div 3 = $ ■ (1 decimal place)

22. Find the value of $78.5 \div 4$ correct to 1 decimal place.

$78.5 \div 4 = $ ■ (1 decimal place)

23. Find the value of each of the following correct to
   1 decimal place.
   (a) $1 \div 6$ (b) $4 \div 7$ (c) $5 \div 9$
   (d) $0.9 \div 4$ (e) $2.5 \div 6$ (f) $43.5 \div 8$

Workbook Exercise 38

24. Ellie bought 5 boxes of cookies for $8.
    How much did two boxes cost?

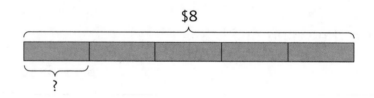

$8 ÷ 5 = $1.60

Each box cost $1.60.

Two boxes cost $1.60 × 2 = ■

25. Taylor has $5.40.
    She has 3 times as much money as Bonita.
    How much more money does Taylor have than Bonita?

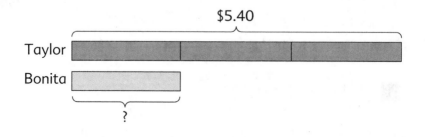

$5.40 ÷ 3 = $1.80

Bonita has $1.80.

$5.40 − $1.80 = $■

Taylor has $■ more than Bonita.

26. Steve bought 5 gal of orange juice.
    After filling up 5 bottles of the same size with orange juice, he had 0.25 gal of orange juice left.
    Find the amount of orange juice in each bottle.

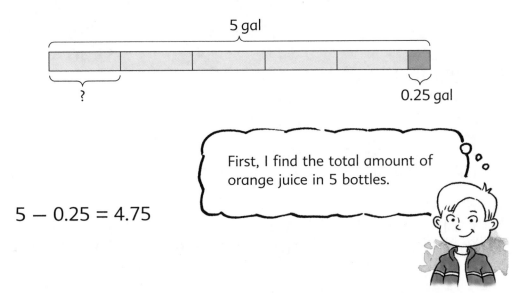

$5 - 0.25 = 4.75$

The total amount of orange juice in 5 bottles was 4.75 gal.

$4.75 \div 5 = \blacksquare$

The amount of orange juice in each bottle was ▓ gal.

27. Mrs. Kim used 4 bags of flour to make 5 cakes of the same size.
    Each bag of flour weighed 1.35 kg.
    How much flour did she use for each cake?

$1.35 \times 4 = 5.4$

4 bags of flour weighed 5.4 kg.

$5.4 \div 5 = \blacksquare$

She used ▓ kg of flour for each cake.

Workbook Exercises 39 & 40

PRACTICE 2D

Find the value of each of the following:

	(a)	(b)	(c)
1.	4 × 8.2	5.29 × 3	8 × 3.29
2.	$0.15 × 6	$4.05 × 4	$3.40 × 9
3.	25.6 ÷ 8	2.94 ÷ 7	6.8 ÷ 5
4.	$0.90 ÷ 6	$4.20 ÷ 7	$6.80 ÷ 8

5. Estimate and then multiply.
   (a) 9 × 4.36   (b) 6 × 5.25   (c) 1.94 × 7

6. Estimate and then divide.
   (a) 5.9 ÷ 2   (b) 23.94 ÷ 6   (c) 35.04 ÷ 4

7. Mrs. King poured 6 qt of syrup equally into 4 bottles.
   How much syrup was there in each bottle?

8. 1 liter of gas weighs 1.25 kg.
   What is the weight of 6 liters of gas?

9. A ribbon 6.75 yd long is cut into 5 equal pieces.
   How long is each piece?

10. Dan spent $3 on string and $1.40 on beads to make
    one pot hanger.
    How much will it cost him to make 4 pot hangers?

11. When a box contains 6 bars of chocolate, it weighs 2.34 kg.
    The box, when empty, weighs 0.06 kg.
    Find the weight of one bar of chocolate.

12. Maria paid $8.25 for a book and a comic.
    The book cost twice as much as the comic.
    Find the cost of the book.

PRACTICE 2E

1. Steve used 8 cans of paint to paint his home.
   Each can contained 5.5 liters of paint.
   How much paint did he use altogether?

2. Mrs. Bates weighs 47.6 kg.
   She is 4 times as heavy as her daughter.
   What is her daughter's weight?

3. A doll costs $4.95.
   A toy robot costs 3 times as much as the doll.
   Find the cost of the toy robot.

4. 3 girls shared the cost of a birthday present equally.
   The birthday present cost $17.40.
   How much did each girl pay?

5. Mr. Friedman bought 5 storybooks at $2.80 each.
   He gave the cashier $20.
   How much change did he receive?

6. Marvin bought 5 m of cloth at a sale.
   He gave the cashier $50 and received $15.25 change.
   Find the cost of 1 m of cloth.

7. Mary saved $25 in 5 days.
   She saved $4.60 a day in the first 4 days.
   How much did she save on the fifth day?

8. 3 cups of tea and a glass of orange juice cost $4.40.
   Each cup of tea cost $0.65.
   Find the cost of the glass of orange juice.

PRACTICE 2F

1. Eric and his friends had 3 plates of fried rice for lunch.
   Each plate of fried rice cost $2.50.
   How much did they pay altogether?

2. Mrs. Lee used 6.6 m of lace for 4 pillow cases.
   If she used an equal length of lace for each pillow case, how much lace did she use for each pillow case?

3. Damon mailed 4 packages.
   One of them weighed 1.8 kg.
   The other 3 packages weighed 2.05 kg each.
   Find the total weight of the 4 packages.

4. Tracy bought a pot and 6 plates.
   The pot cost $5.65.
   Each plate cost $1.45.
   How much did she spend altogether?

5. Natalie and Alice shared the cost of their lunch equally.
   The lunch cost $6.70.
   How much money did Alice have left if she had $15.35 at first?

6. Janet bought 3 pencils and a pen for $2.20.
   If the pen cost $0.85, how much did each pencil cost?

7. Mrs. Dunn sewed curtains for her living room and 3 bedrooms.
   She used 3.46 m of material for each bedroom and 4.25 m of material for the living room.
   How much material did she use altogether?

8. The usual price of a kiwi is $0.60.
   At a sale, a packet of 4 kiwis is sold for $2.20.
   How much cheaper is a kiwi at the sale?

REVIEW B

1. (a) What number is 0.1 more than 124.56?
   (b) What number is 0.01 more than 124.56?
   (c) What number is 0.1 less than 124.56?
   (d) What number is 0.01 less than 124.56?

2. Write **>** (is greater than), **<** (is less than) or **=** (is equal to) in place of each ☐.

   (a) $4\frac{3}{5}$ ☐ 4.35

   (b) $2\frac{2}{50}$ ☐ 2.2

   (c) 14.09 ☐ $14\frac{1}{10}$

   (d) $7\frac{3}{20}$ ☐ 7.15

3. Write the missing number in each ■.

   (a) $4.12 = 4 + \frac{1}{10} + \frac{2}{■}$

   (b) $1.08 = \frac{■}{100}$

   (c) $5.7 = 5 + \frac{7}{■}$

   (d) $39.16 = 39 + \frac{■}{10} + \frac{6}{100}$

4. Find the value of each of the following:

   (a) $\frac{1}{2}$ of 200

   (b) $\frac{1}{4}$ of $140

   (c) $\frac{1}{3}$ of 27 kg

   (d) $\frac{1}{5}$ of 50 m

5. Estimate and then multiply.
   (a) 4.9×6
   (b) 8.9×7
   (c) 3.99×5
   (d) 10.99×3

6. What is the value of the digit **8** in each of the following?
   (a) 3**8**,157   (b) 45**8**3   (c) 12,4**3**8   (d) **8**9,015

7. Which one of the following has 6 as a factor?

   61,   36,   56,   76

8. The product of two numbers is 456.
   If one of the numbers is 8, what is the other number?

9. Find the sum of +

   (a) $\frac{1}{3}$ and $\frac{9}{12}$

   (b) $\frac{1}{3}$ and $\frac{5}{9}$

   (c) $\frac{5}{6}$ and $\frac{1}{2}$

   (d) $\frac{4}{5}$ and $\frac{7}{10}$

10. Find the difference between ~

    (a) $\frac{11}{12}$ and $\frac{1}{4}$

    (b) 3 and $\frac{3}{7}$

    (c) $\frac{1}{2}$ and $\frac{1}{8}$

    (d) 6 and $\frac{1}{6}$

11. Arrange the numbers in increasing order.

    (a) $\frac{1}{3}$, $\frac{5}{6}$, $\frac{1}{12}$

    (b) $1\frac{3}{4}$, $\frac{9}{4}$, $1\frac{1}{4}$

    (c) $1\frac{3}{5}$, $\frac{9}{2}$, 3

    (d) $2\frac{1}{5}$, $\frac{9}{4}$, $\frac{20}{6}$

12. Mr. Reed sold his car for $35,950.
    Round off this amount of money to the nearest $100.

13. David bought a kettle for $76.90.
    Round off this amount of money to the nearest dollar.

14. Divide. Give each answer as a decimal correct to
    1 decimal place.
    (a) 20 ÷ 3   (b) 100 ÷ 7   (c) 39 ÷ 8

15. The area of a rectangle is 50 cm².
    If the length of the rectangle is 10 cm, find its width.

16. The perimeter of a square is 36 in.
    Find the length of one side of the square.

17. A cup of coffee cost $0.65.
    David ordered 6 cups of coffee.
    How much did he pay?

18. A ribbon 4.8 m long is cut into 8 equal pieces.
    What is the length of each piece?

19. Juan painted $\frac{3}{10}$ of a pole red.

    The rest of the pole was **not** painted.
    What fraction of the pole was **not** painted?

20. Find the perimeter of a square garden if each side of the

    garden is $\frac{3}{5}$ km long.

21. Mary cut a cake into 16 equal pieces.

    If she gave $\frac{3}{8}$ of the cake to her friend, how many pieces of
    cake did she give away?

22. 200 children took part in a fire drill.
    $\frac{5}{8}$ of them were boys.
    How many girls were there?

23. A bucket can hold 6 liters of water.

    If it is $\frac{3}{4}$ full, how many liters of water does it contain?

24. Ashley saved a total of $1800 in 12 months.
    She saved $157 a month in the first 11 months.
    How much did she save in the twelfth month?

25. Roger has $58.70.
    He wants to buy a radio and a watch.
    The watch costs $35.90 and the radio costs $28.50.
    How much more money does he need?

3 Measures

1 Multiplication

The 3 packages are of the same weight.
Each of them weighs 1 kg 200 g.
What is the total weight of the 3 packages?

1 kg 200 g × 3 = ■ kg ■ g

The total weight of the 3 packages is ■ kg ■ g.

1. The distance around a track in a park was 1 km 300 m. Ali ran round the track 4 times. How far did he run?

   1 km 300 m × 4 = ■ km ■ m

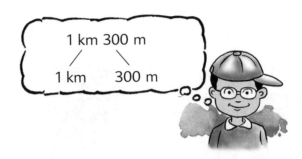

   He ran ■ km ■ m.

2. Gerald filled a tank with 5 buckets of water.
   Each bucket contained 2 ℓ 400 ml of water.
   What was the capacity of the tank?

   2 ℓ 400 ml × 5 = ■ ℓ ■ ml
         = ■ ℓ

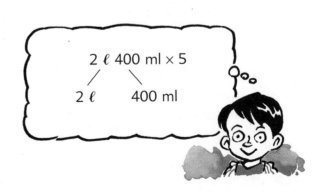

   The capacity of the bucket was ■ ℓ.

2 Division

Jane cut a ribbon 5 m 20 cm long into 4 equal pieces to make flowers. What was the length of each piece?

5 m 20 cm ÷ 4 = ▮ m ▮ cm

The length of each piece was ▮ m ▮ cm.

1. A box contains 5 bags of flour.
   If the total weight of the flour is 5 kg 650 g, find the weight of each bag of flour.

   5 kg 650 g ÷ 5 = 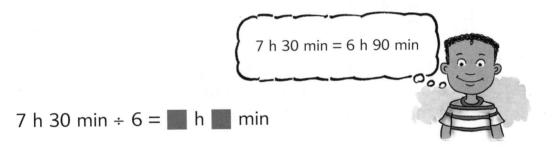 kg ▪ g

   The weight of each bag of flour is ▪ kg ▪ g.

Workbook Exercise 41

2. A tailor took 7 hours 30 minutes to sew 6 shirts. How long did she take to sew one shirt?

   7 h 30 min = 6 h 90 min

   7 h 30 min ÷ 6 = ▪ h ▪ min

   She took ▪ hours ▪ minutes to sew one shirt.

3. Marina poured 3 ℓ 200 ml of milk equally into 8 glasses. How many milliliters of milk were there in each glass?

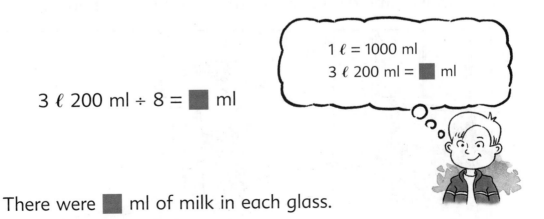

   1 ℓ = 1000 ml
   3 ℓ 200 ml = ▪ ml

   3 ℓ 200 ml ÷ 8 = ▪ ml

   There were ▪ ml of milk in each glass.

PRACTICE 3A

1. Multiply in compound units.
   (a) 3 km 200 m × 5
   (b) 4 ℓ 300 ml × 4
   (c) 2 h 20 min × 5
   (d) 5 kg 200 g × 3
   (e) 6 m 20 cm × 6
   (f) 3 yd 2 ft × 7

2. Divide in compound units.
   (a) 2 ℓ 240 ml ÷ 2
   (b) 5 km 300 m ÷ 2
   (c) 1 h 30 min ÷ 5
   (d) 4 kg 500 g ÷ 3
   (e) 2 m 60 cm ÷ 4
   (f) 4 ft 3 in. ÷ 3

3. Mrs. Gray used 2 bottles of syrup to make drinks.
   Each bottle contained 1 ℓ 275 ml of syrup.
   How much syrup did she use?

4. Ian bought 3 kg 570 g of beans.
   He packed them equally into 3 bags.
   What was the weight of the beans in each bag?

5. Henry spent 3 hours 30 minutes every morning to paint his house.
   He finished painting his whole house in 5 mornings.
   How much time did he spend to paint his whole house?

6. A pineapple weighs 1 kg 800 g.
    A watermelon is 3 times as heavy as the pineapple.
    (a) What is the weight of the watermelon?
    (b) What is the total weight of the two fruits?

7. Morgan works 8 hours 30 minutes everyday in a factory.
    She is paid $5 each hour.
    (a) How many hours does she work for 6 days?
    (b) How much does she earn for 6 days?

8. A piece of rope 3 m 66 cm long was cut into 2 pieces.
    The longer piece was twice as long as the shorter piece. What
    was the length of the longer piece?

9. Hillary used 2 bags of sugar to make 8 cakes.
    One bag contained 1 kg 240 g of sugar and the other contained
    1 kg 160 g of sugar.
    If she used the same amount of sugar for each cake, how much
    sugar did she use for each cake?

10. A meter of ribbon cost $4. Mary bought 2 pieces of ribbon each
     of length 3 m 50 cm. How much did she pay for the 2 pieces of
     ribbon?

Symmetry

1 ## Symmetric Figures

Many things around us have **symmetry**.
Here are some of them.

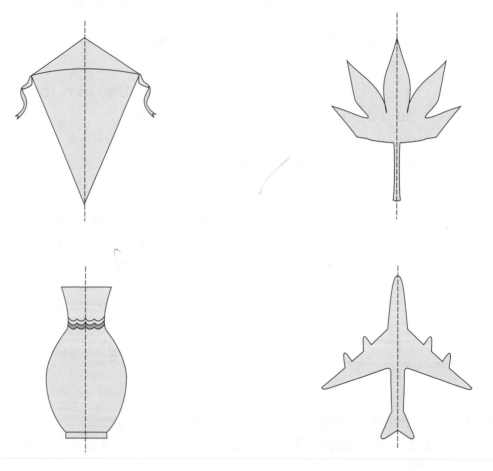

These are **symmetric figures**.
The dotted line in each figure
is **a line of symmetry**.

Look for some more examples of symmetry around you.

1. Fold a piece of paper.
   Cut out a figure which starts and ends on the fold line like this:

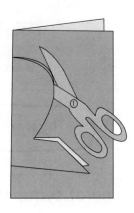

   Unfold the figure.
   You will get a symmetric figure.

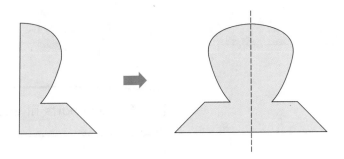

   The fold line is a line of symmetry.

2. Draw and cut out some symmetric figures.

(a)

(b)

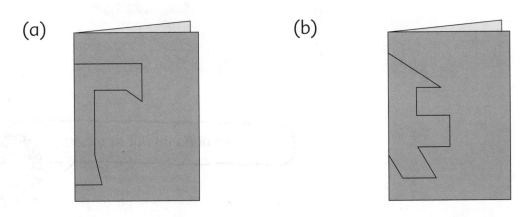

Workbook Exercise 42

3. Fold each rectangle along the dotted line as shown.

(a)

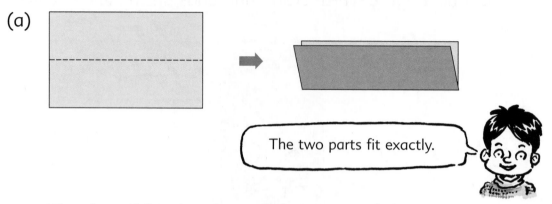

The two parts fit exactly.

The dotted line is a line of symmetry of the rectangle.

(b)

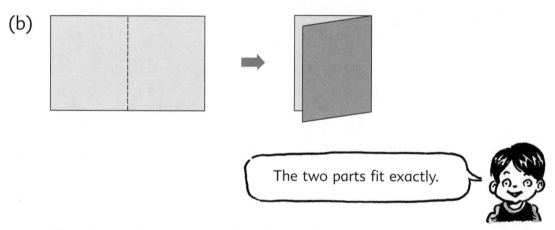

The two parts fit exactly.

The dotted line is another line of symmetry of the rectangle.

(c)

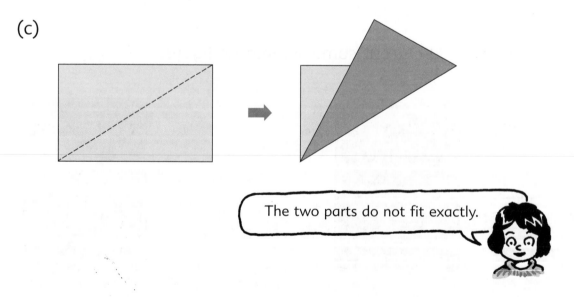

The two parts do not fit exactly.

The dotted line is not a line of symmetry of the rectangle.

4. (a) An isosceles triangle is a triangle with two equal sides.

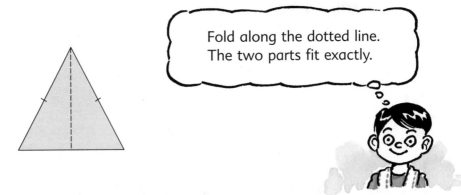

Fold along the dotted line.
The two parts fit exactly.

The dotted line is a line of symmetry of the triangle.

    (b) An equilateral triangle is a triangle with three equal sides.

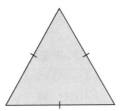

Draw a line of symmetry of the triangle.

5. The following triangles have a right angle. They are called right-angled triangles.

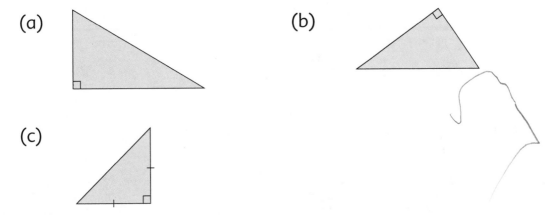

(a)

(b)

(c)

Which one of the above right-angled triangles has a line of symmetry?

6. (a) A parallelogram is a 4-sided figure with two pairs of parallel sides.

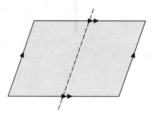

Is the dotted line a line of symmetry?

(b) The following parallelogram has 4 equal sides. It is called a rhombus.

Is the dotted line a line of symmetry?

7. Each of the following 4-sided figures has only one pair of parallel sides.
It is called a trapezoid.

(a)

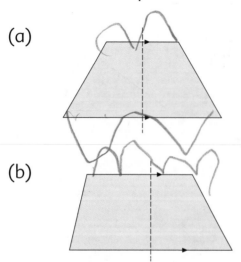

(b)

Is the dotted line a line of symmetry in each trapezoid?

8. In each of the following figures, is the dotted line a line of symmetry?

(a)

(b)

(c)

(d)

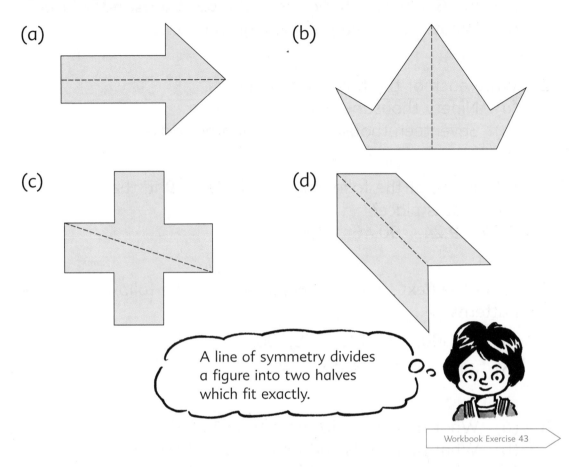

A line of symmetry divides a figure into two halves which fit exactly.

Workbook Exercise 43

9. Draw this half of a symmetric figure on a square grid.

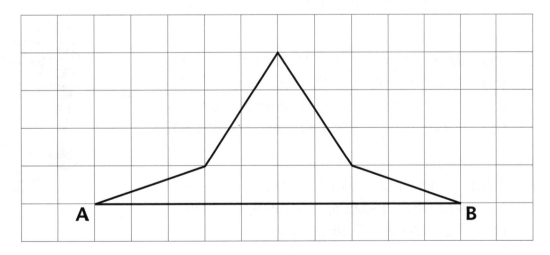

Then complete the symmetric figure with AB as a line of symmetry.

Workbook Exercise 44

REVIEW C

1. (a) In 26,085, which digit is in the **ten thousands** place?
   (b) What is the value of the digit **3** in 5.2**3**?

2. Write each of the following in figures.
   (a) Ninety thousand, five hundred four
   (b) Seventeen thousand, five hundred forty-one

3. Which one of the following has the digit **9** in the hundredths place?
   2.6**9**, **9**.24, **9**0.46, **9**00.5

4. Write the next two numbers in each of the following number patterns.
   (a) 74,300, 76,300, 78,300, ▢, ▢
   (b) 4.09, 4.59, 5.09, ▢, ▢

5. (a) What number is 10 more than 14,670?
   (b) What number is 1000 more than 29,083?
   (c) What number is 100 less than 10,000?
   (d) What number is 1000 less than 90,301?

6. (a) What number is 0.1 more than 6.93?
   (b) What number is 0.1 less than 5?
   (c) What number is 0.01 more than 2.4?
   (d) What number is 0.01 less than 3.612?

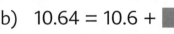

7. Arrange the numbers in increasing order.
   (a) 41,508, 14,058, 14,508, 41,058
   (b) 72, 24.3, 0.96, 8.54

8. What is the missing number in each ▢?
   (a) 6.28 = 6 + ▢   (b) 10.64 = 10.6 + ▢

9. What number does each letter represent?

(a)

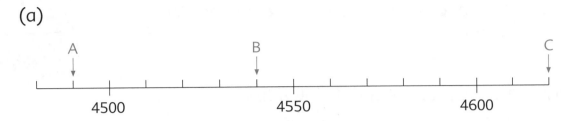

4500　　　4550　　　4600

(b)

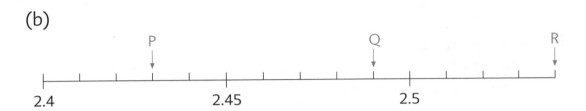

2.4　　　2.45　　　2.5

10. Round off 8.45 to 1 decimal place.

11. (a) Write down two factors of 45.
    (b) Write down a common multiple of 8 and 6.

12. (a) Find the sum of 3.09, 5.92 and 1.4.
    (b) Find the product of 24 and 639.

13. The difference between two numbers is 2790.
    If the smaller number is 3560, what is the other number?

14. A blue ribbon is 1242 in. long.
    It is 9 times as long as a red ribbon.
    How long is the red ribbon?

15. Claire bought 6 cans of milk.
    Each can of milk cost $1.25.
    How much did she spend?

16. The capacity of a bottle is 1.5 qt.
    It is filled with 0.75 qt of water.
    How much more water can be poured into
    the bottle?

17. Peter drinks 125 ml of milk a day.
    How much milk does he drink in two weeks?
    (Give the answer in liters and milliliters.)

18. Carlos had $50.
    He spent $11.90 on a book and $27.35 on a tennis racket.
    How much money did he have left?

19. Sara saved $20.35.
    Her brother saved $16.85 more than she.
    How much did they save altogether?

20. Miss Chen and 18 students went on a picnic.
    They spent $72 altogether.
    Each of the students paid $3.
    Miss Chen paid the rest.
    How much did Miss Chen pay?

21. Robert bought a washing machine and 3 microwave ovens
    for $2000.
    The washing machine cost $665.
    How much did each microwave oven cost?

22. The cost of renting a car is $4500 a month.
    4 friends rented a car for 2 months.
    They shared the cost equally.
    How much did each person pay?

REVIEW D

1.

| 251.83 | 132.85 |
| 123.58 | 135.28 |

   (a)   Write the numbers in increasing order.
   (b)   What is the value of the digit 2 in each number?
   (c)   In which number does the digit 5 stand for 5 tenths?

2.   (a)   In 5630, which digit is in the **hundreds** place?
   (b)   In 12.78, which digit is in the **tenths** place?

3.   Write each of the following as a decimal.

   (a) $400 + 50 + 0.07$

   (b) $30 + 5 + \dfrac{5}{10} + \dfrac{3}{100}$

   (c) $30 + 0.5 + 0.04$

   (d) $100 + 7 + 0.08$

4.   This graph shows the number of children in 6 art classes.

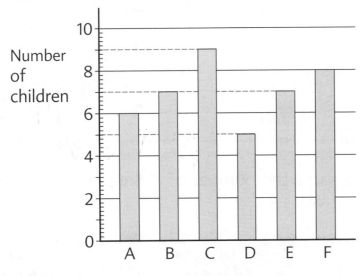

   Find the total number of children in the 6 art classes.

5.   Estimate and then multiply.
   (a) 456×60 (b) 306×27 (c) 783×41

6. Find the value of each of the following:

    (a) $\dfrac{2}{3} + \dfrac{7}{9}$

    (b) $2 - \dfrac{5}{8}$

    (c) $\dfrac{4}{5} + \dfrac{3}{5}$

    (d) $\dfrac{7}{8} - \dfrac{3}{4}$

    (e) $\dfrac{5}{6} \times 60$

    (f) $\dfrac{3}{4} \times 6$

7. (a) Express 1.36 as a fraction in its simplest form.

   (b) Express $3\dfrac{11}{50}$ as a decimal.

8. This table shows the amount of money Susan spent in 5 days.

Monday	Tuesday	Wednesday	Thursday	Friday
$3.45	$2.05	$2	$3.60	$1.15

   Find the total amount of money she spent in 5 days.

9. Find the perimeter and area of each figure. (All lines meet at right angles.)

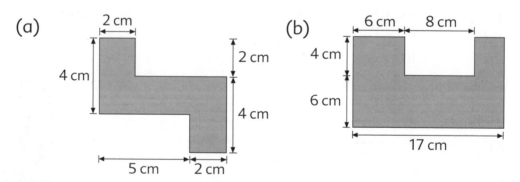

(a) 2 cm   4 cm   2 cm   4 cm   5 cm   2 cm

(b) 6 cm   8 cm   4 cm   6 cm   17 cm

10. The cards below show the number of children who took part in three different activities.

Walkathon 56 boys 50 girls	Swimming competition 63 boys 66 girls	Carnival 45 boys 47 girls

    (a) Make a table to show the data.
    (b) Find the total number of children in the three activities.

11. The perimeter of a rectangle is 42 in.
    If the length of the rectangle is 12 in., find its width.

12. The area of a square flower bed is 25 m².
    Find its perimeter.

13. (a) How many milliliters must be added to 660 ml to make
        1 liter?

    (b) How many grams must be added to 256 g to make 1 kg?

    (c) How many inches must be added to 7 in. to make 1 ft?

14. (a) A shop is open from 11:25 a.m. to 7 p.m.
        How long is the shop open?

    (b) A film show started at 7:50 p.m.
        It lasted 2 hours 15 minutes.
        When did the show end?

15. Terry had $34.

    He spent $\frac{2}{5}$ of the money on a picture book.

    Then he spent $8.25 on a birthday present.
    How much money did he spend altogether?

16. After spending $\frac{3}{5}$ of his money on a tennis racket,

    Shawn had $14 left.
    How much did the tennis racket cost?

Solid Figures

1 Identifying Solid Figures

The drawing of a cube is shown below.

Cube

We can draw a cube in other ways.

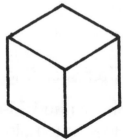

1. This is the drawing of a unit cube on a dotted paper.

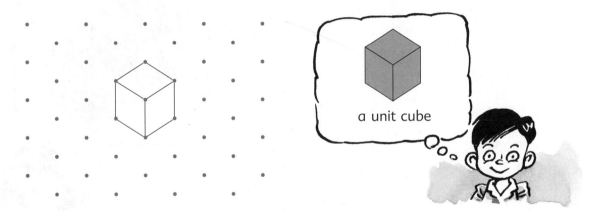

a unit cube

When another unit cube is added to it, we get:

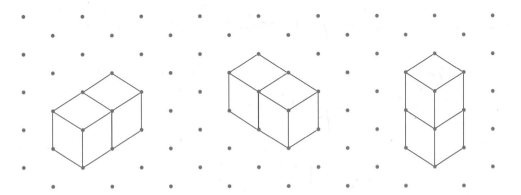

Each of these solids is made up of 2 unit cubes.

2. (a) Use 4 unit cubes to build a solid like this:

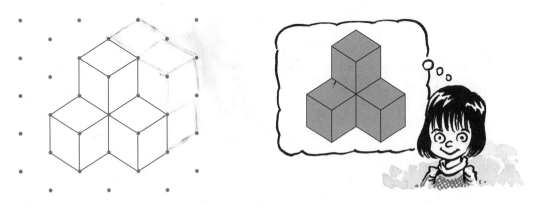

   (b) Build a different solid with 4 unit cubes.

3. Use 8 unit cubes to build a bigger cube.

Workbook Exercise 45

4. Use unit cubes to build this cuboid.

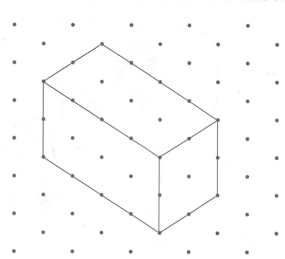

How many unit cubes are needed to build the cuboid?

5. Use unit cubes to build each of the following solids.

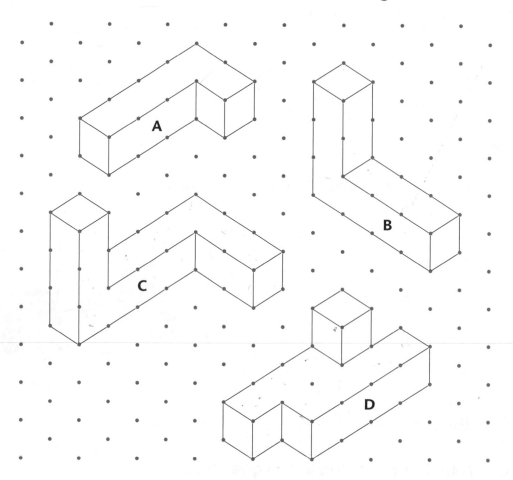

How many cubes are needed to build each of the solids?

6. How many unit cubes are needed to build each of the following solids?

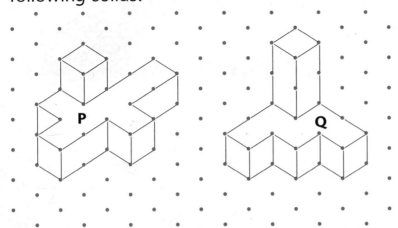

Workbook Exercise 46

7. Use unit cubes to build cuboid A.
Then remove some unit cubes to get the solid B.
How many cubes are removed?

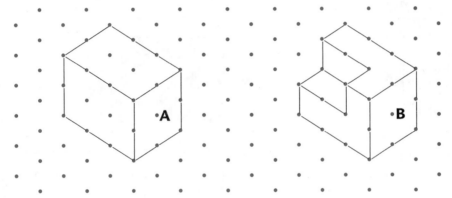

8. Use unit cubes to build solid C.
Then add some unit cubes to get solid D.
How many cubes are added?

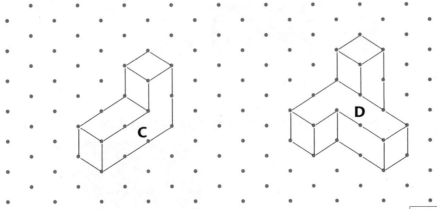

Workbook Exercise 47

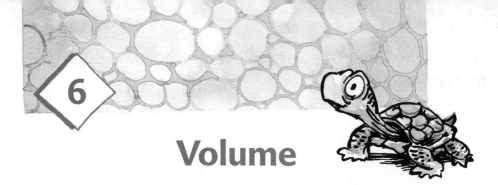

Volume

1 ## Cubic Units

> The **volume** of a solid is the amount of space it occupies.

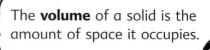

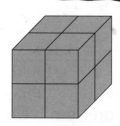

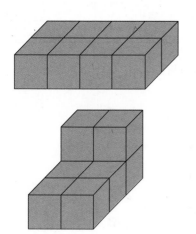

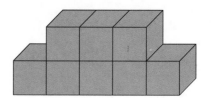

These solids have the same volume. The volume of each solid is 8 cubic units.

> The volume of a unit cube is 1 **cubic unit**.

1.   Use 6 unit cubes to build a solid like this:

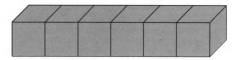

Its volume is 6 cubic units.

Rearrange the 6 cubes to build another solid like this:

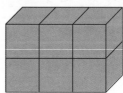

Its volume is ■ cubic units.

2. What is the volume of each of the following solids?
    Which solid has the greatest volume?

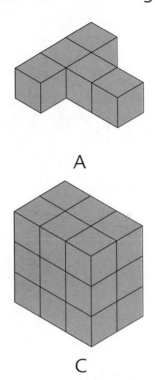

A

B

C

D

Workbook Exercise 48

3. The figure shows a 1-cm cube.
    Each edge of the cube is 1 cm long.
    The volume of the cube is 1 **cubic centimeter (cm³)**.

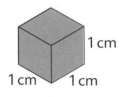

1 cm

1 cm   1 cm

The cubic centimeter (cm³) is
a unit of volume.

Use 2 pieces of 1-cm cubes to build this solid:

.The volume of the solid is 2 cm³.

91

Add another 1-cm cube to build this solid:

The volume of the solid is ■ cm³.

How many 1-cm cubes are needed to build this solid?

The volume of the solid is ■ cm³.

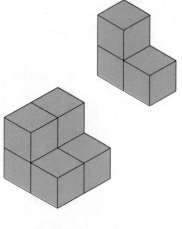

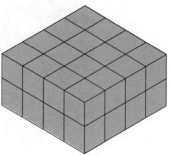

4. The cuboid is made up of 1-cm cubes. Find its volume.

5. The following solids are made up of 1-cm cubes. Find the volume of each solid.

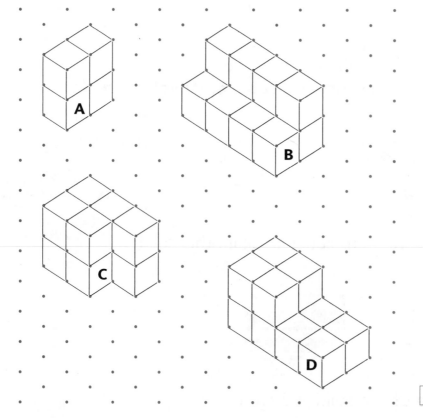

Workbook Exercise 49

2 Volume of a Cuboid

The cuboid is made up of 1-cm cubes.

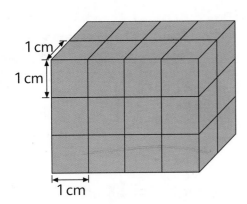

1 cm
1 cm
1 cm

$4 \times 2 = 8$
There are 8 cubes in each layer.

$8 \times 3 = 24$
There are 24 cubes altogether.

The length of the cuboid is 4 cm.

Its width is 2 cm.

Its height is 3 cm.

Its volume is ⬛ cm³.

$4 \times 2 \times 3$

The cuboid measures 4 cm by 2 cm by 3 cm.

1 cm
1 cm
1 cm

3 cm
2 cm
4 cm

Volume of cuboid = Length × Width × Height

1. The following cuboids are made up of 1-cm cubes.
   Find the length, width, height and volume of each cuboid.

(a)

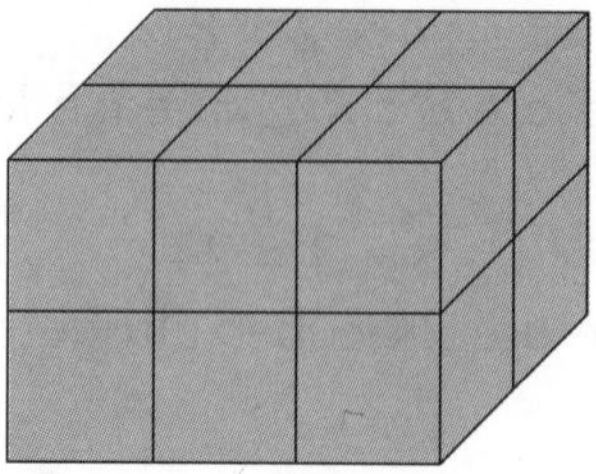

Length = ▇ cm

Width = ▇ cm

Height = ▇ cm

Volume = ▇ cm³

(b)

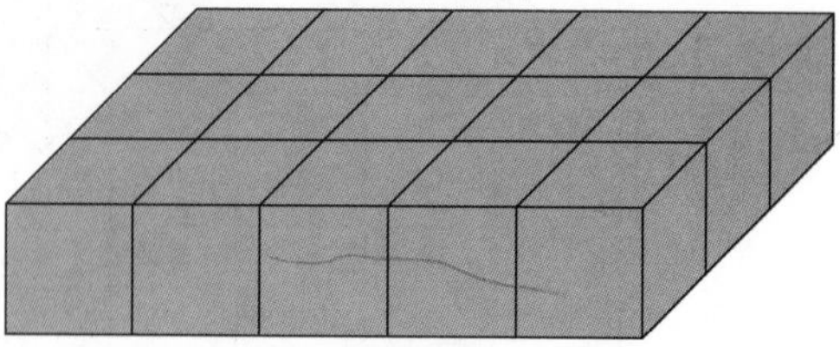

Length = ▇ cm

Width = ▇ cm

Height = ▇ cm

Volume = ▇ cm³

(c)

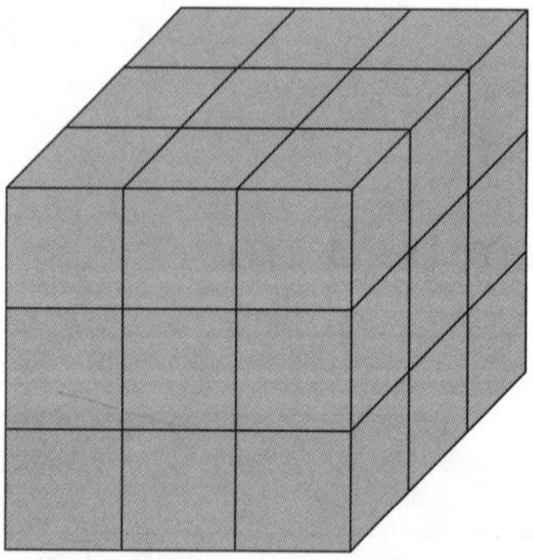

(d)

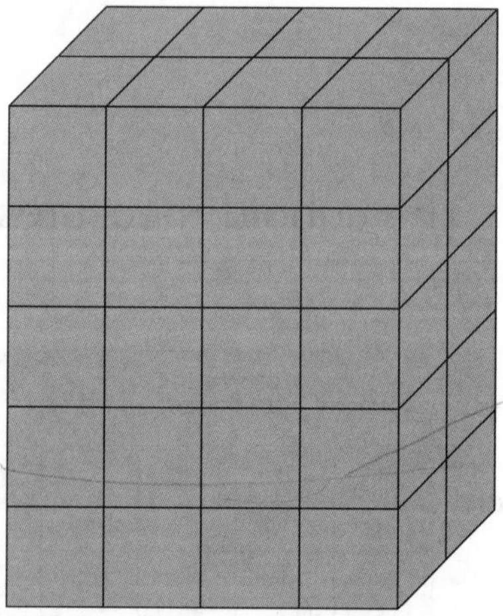

Length = ▇ cm

Width = ▇ cm

Height = ▇ cm

Volume = ▇ cm³

Length = ▇ cm

Width = ▇ cm

Height = ▇ cm

Volume = ▇ cm³

2. The cuboid measures 8 in. by 2 in. by 5 in.
   Find its volume.

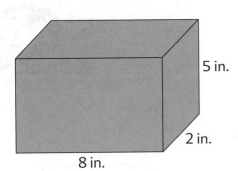

How many pieces of 1-in. cubes are needed to build this cuboid?

$8 \times 2 \times 5 = $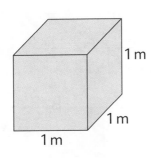

The volume of the cuboid is ▪ in.³

3. The figure shows a cube of edge 1 m.
   The volume of the cube is 1 **cubic meter (m³)**.

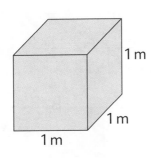

The cubic meter (m³) is also a unit of volume.

What is the volume of a cuboid which measures 2 m by 1 m by 1 m?

$2 \times 1 \times 1 = $ ▪

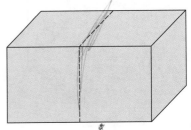

The volume of the cuboid is ▪ m³.

4. Find the volume of a cuboid which measures 5 m by 3 m by 4 m.

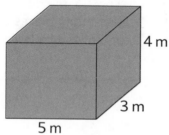

5. Find the volume of a cube of edge 3 m.

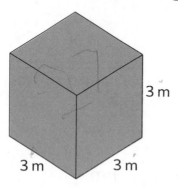

6. Find the volume of each of the following cuboids.

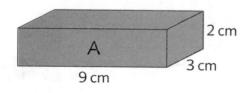

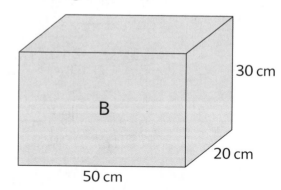

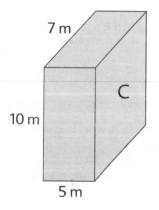

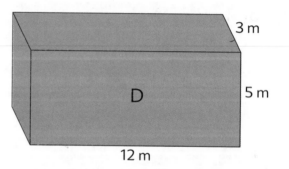

Workbook Exercise 50

7. The rectangular box measures 10 cm by 10 cm by 10 cm.
   It can hold 1 liter of water.

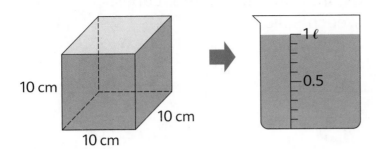

Volume of water in the box = $10 \times 10 \times 10$

$$= \blacksquare \ cm^3$$

$1 \ \ell = \blacksquare \ cm^3$

$1 \ ml = \blacksquare \ cm^3$

$1 \ \ell = 1000 \ ml$

8. Write in cubic centimeters.
   (a) 2 ℓ   (b) 400 ml   (c) 1 ℓ 200 ml

9. Write in liters and milliliters.
   (a) 1750 cm³   (b) 2450 cm³   (c) 3050 cm³

10. A rectangular fish tank measures 30 cm by 20 cm by 20 cm.
    (a) Find its capacity in cubic centimeters.
    (b) If the tank is filled with water to a depth of 8 cm, find the
        volume of the water in liters and milliliters.
        (1 ℓ = 1000 cm³)

   (a) Capacity of the tank
       = $30 \times 20 \times 20$
       = $\blacksquare \ cm^3$

   (b) Volume of water
       = $30 \times 20 \times 8$
       = $\blacksquare \ cm^3$
       = $\blacksquare \ \ell \ \blacksquare \ ml$

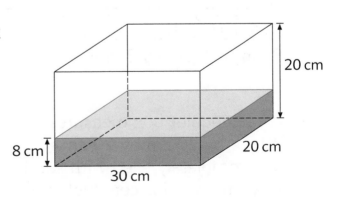

Workbook Exercise 51

PRACTICE 6A

1. The following solids are made up of 1-in. cubes. Find the volume of each solid.

   (a) 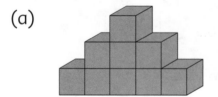   (b)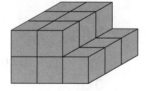

2. A cuboid measures 30 cm by 25 cm by 15 cm. Find its volume.

   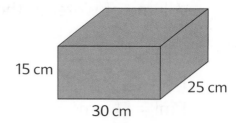

3. Find the volume of a cube of edge 5 cm.

   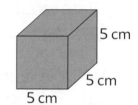

4. A rectangular tank is 12 ft long, 10 ft wide and 3 ft high. Find its capacity in cubic feet.

   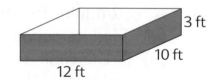

5. How many 1-cm cubes are needed to build a cuboid measuring 8 cm by 5 cm by 3 cm?

   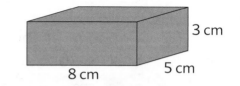

6. A rectangular box measures 30 cm by 20 cm by 20 cm. It is completely filled with sand. How many cubic centimeters of sand are there in the box?

   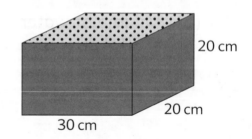

PRACTICE 6B

1. Write in cubic centimeters.
   (a) 3 ℓ
   (b) 250 ml
   (c) 2 ℓ 60 ml

2. Write in liters and milliliters.
   (a) 1050 cm³
   (b) 1800 cm³
   (c) 3500 cm³

3. A rectangular tin measures 15 cm by 10 cm by 3 cm.
   How many milliliters of water can it hold?
   (1 ml = 1 cm³)

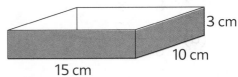

4. A rectangular tank 20 cm long, 18 cm wide and 20 cm high
   is filled with water to a depth of 8 cm.
   (a) Find the volume of water in
       cubic centimeters.
   (b) Express the volume of water
       in liters and milliliters.
       (1 ℓ = 1000 cm³)

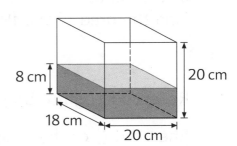

5. How many cubic centimeters of water are there in each of the
   following containers?

   (a)   (b)

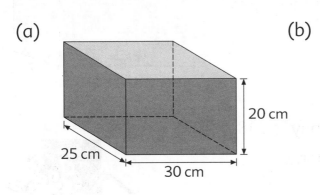

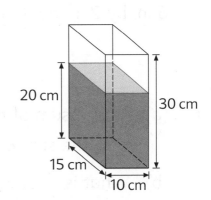

REVIEW E

1. Arrange the numbers in increasing order.
    (a) 80,431, 79,431, 80,331, 79,433
    (b) 0.6, 0.55, 0.7, 0.09

    (c) $2\frac{2}{9}$, $\frac{9}{2}$, $2\frac{2}{3}$, $2\frac{4}{9}$

2. Find the value of each of the following. Give the answer in its simplest form.

    (a) $\frac{5}{8} + \frac{5}{8}$ (b) $\frac{2}{3} + \frac{5}{9}$ (c) $5 - \frac{3}{10}$

    (d) $\frac{5}{6} - \frac{2}{3}$ (e) $\frac{2}{7} \times 28$ (f) $16 \times \frac{5}{6}$

3. The figure shows a rectangular field which measures 25 m by 20 m. There is a rectangular flower bed at the center of the field. Find the area of the flower bed.

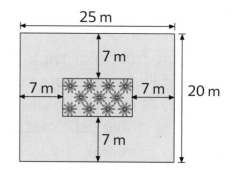

4. Rebecca bought a bag of flour which weighed 600 g.

    She used $\frac{3}{5}$ of the flour to bake a cake.
    How many grams of flour did she use?

5. How many 1-in. cubes are needed to build a cuboid which measures 6 in. by 2 in. by 3 in.?

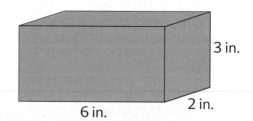

6. (a) $\frac{2}{3}$ of a sum of money is $18.
        Find the sum of money.

    (b) What is $\frac{1}{4}$ of 32?

7. (a) Express $1\frac{3}{5}$ as a decimal.

(b) Express 2.05 as a fraction in its simplest form.

8. Estimate and then multiply.
   (a) 5637×4 (b) 66×582 (c) 295×49

9. The figure shows a cuboid A that is made up of unit cubes. How many unit cubes are removed from the cuboid A to get solid B?

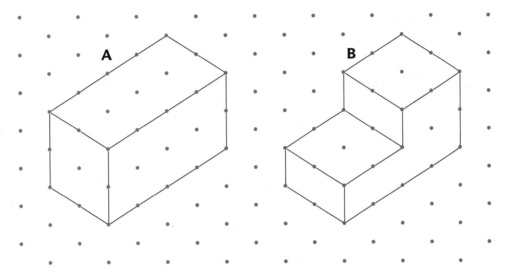

10. Solid A is made up of unit cubes.

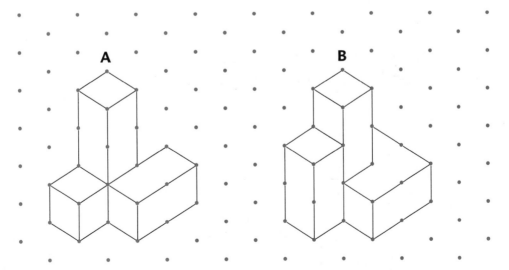

(a) How many unit cubes are needed to build A?
(b) How many unit cubes are added to solid A to get solid B?

11. Copy and complete the symmetric figure.
    (The dotted line is a line of symmetry.)

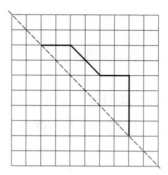

12. Copy and draw a line of symmetry of the symmetric figure.

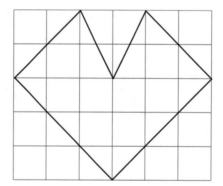

13. Copy and complete the symmetric figure.
    (The dotted line is a line of symmetry.)

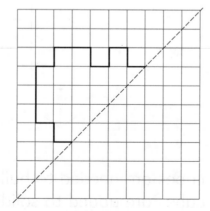

14. Which one of the following is a pair of parallel lines?

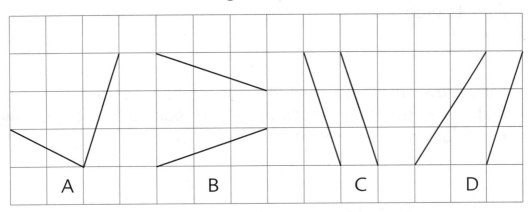

A   B   C   D

15. Find the perimeter and area of each figure. (All lines meet at right angles.)

(a)

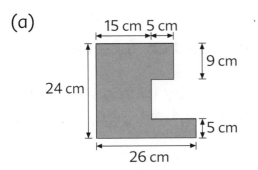

(b)

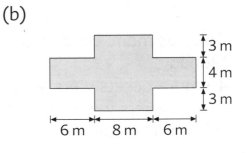

16. Find the area of the shaded part of each rectangle.

(a)

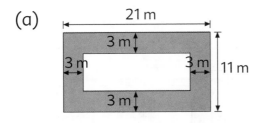

(b)

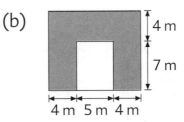

17. Find the length and perimeter of the rectangle.

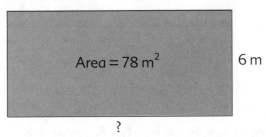

Area = 78 m²   6 m

?

18. The perimeter of a square is 48 in.
    Find its area.

19. Mrs. Brown used 4.5 m of lace for 5 pillow cases.
    If she used an equal length of lace for each pillow case, how much lace did she use for each pillow case?

20. Diana saved $70.50 in 5 weeks.
    If she saved an equal amount each week, how much would she save in 8 weeks?

21. Twice as many concert tickets were sold on Tuesday as on Monday.
    40 more tickets were sold on Wednesday than on Tuesday.
    If 200 tickets were sold on Wednesday, how many tickets were sold on Monday?

22. This graph shows John's savings in five months.

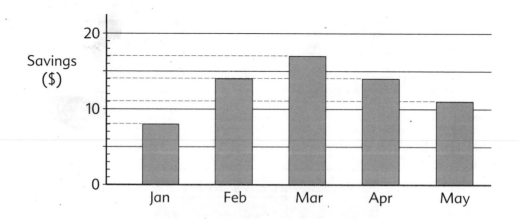

    (a) How much did John save in January?
    (b) In which month did he save the most?
    (c) Find his total savings in the 5 months.

104